D0354518

Warriors Forever

Warriors Forever

JGC/United Publishing Corps Books
http://jgcunited.com

The First Forest by John Gile
Kiss The Sky by Dale Greenlee
Keeping First Things First by John Gile
Just Shades of Brown by Lana Duncan-Hartgraves
What Is That Thing? Whose Stuff Is This? by John Gile
Goodbye, Geraldine by Robert Morgan
Blame It On the System by Tony Lamia
Oh, How I Wished I Could Read! by John Gile
At the Crossroads: A Vision of Hope by Thomas Doran

Patti Terranova
Jon Stenholm

Warriors Forever

John Gile

To Ben Canter,
— I hope you
enjoy the
Rockford Memories,
John Gile
7.15.17

Cover design by Renie Gile

Warriors Forever

John Gile

10 9 8 7 6 5 4 3 2 1

Copyright 2017 by John Gile

Library of Congress Card Number: 2016920012
ISBN: 978-0-910941-37-2

Printed in the United States of America
by Rockford Litho, Rockford, Illinois

In memory of
Alice Saudargas,
whose courage and commitment
to family and community
have made her the consummate
Warrior Forever.

Warriors Forever

Acknowledgements

So many have helped directly and indirectly in the research and writing of *Warriors Forever* that it is impossible to thank everyone here for their support and cooperation. Included among those who lived the legend or have helped create *Warriors Forever* by preserving and sharing their memories of the story are:

Alice Saudargas and the Saudargas family for sharing memories.

Warrior players for hours of interviews in person, by phone, and by email and for giving me access to scrapbooks for as long as needed.

Rockford Register Star Executive Editor Linda Grist Cunningham for permission to use Register Star photos.

Sportswriters, newspapers, and press associations in Chicago, Champaign, Elgin, Danville, Dixon, Rockford, Aurora, Rock Falls, Sterling, and other Illinois cities reporting on the Warriors. (Any omitted credit for unattributed scrapbook clippings called to the publisher's attention will be added in the next edition of *Warriors Forever*.)

Donna Paladino for volunteering to transcribe hours of recorded interviews with players and others.

Michael Golden and Webbs Norman for providing encouragement over breakfasts. Bill and Julie Snively, Annie Miller, and Bruce and Joanne Johnson for reviewing and responding to texts.

Ron Johnson of Rockford Public School District 205, producer of "So Long Sweet Sixteen" 1955 Warrior Documentary.

Countless West High and East High athletes and graduates who shared memories from scrapbooks and in meetings, interviews, and casual conversations.

Friends of West High members who have helped preserve the schools' legacy through the years, including Connie Aarhus, Tina Angileri, Donna Beck, Polly Berg, Edward Conklin, Michael Fahy, Kay and Tom Glenny, Michael Golden, Peg Goral, Bev Graham, Carla Harms, Deanna Hartenberg, Perky and Jay Heath, Marion and Ron Heinen, Larry Johns, David McClelland, Carol and Rex Parker, Carole Rose, Alice Saudargas, Scott and Tom Schwalbach, Glenda Shaver, Michael Smith, and Tyler Smith.

Internet sources, including the Illinois High School Association, historical and public record sites, government sites, and obituary archives. Illinois sportswriters and other journalists, some of whose bylines were on stories in disintegrating clippings, including Charles Bartlett, Byron Baxter, Sue Beckenbaugh, Bert Bertine, Paul Cahill, Dave Condon, Jack Egan, William Gleason, Charles Johnson, Jim Johnston, Warren Kellogg, Bob Lahendio, Roger Lane, Ira Larvey, Ray Lloyd, Dick Lundeen, Kay Meurlott, Bud Nangle, Dave Nightingale, Mark Novak, Cooper Rollow, Bill Schrader, Don Scott, Dick Schwarzlose, T. O. White, Hal Yegli, Isabel Culhane, Dave Albee, Pat Cunningham, Judy Emerson, and Frank Schier.

Warriors Forever production underwriters, including Sue and Sherwood Anderson, Ann Marlow Armstrong, John Bell, Jim Bennett, Bette and Rease Binger, Sue Ellen and Rod Coffman, Sue Beckenbaugh Duesler, and Barbara Gentry, Kay and Tom Glenny, Deb and Mike Golden, Don Grabow, Perky and Jay Heath, Pat Karp, Tom and Leslie Kiloren, Kathy and David McClelland, Sharon and Edward McClelland, Barb and Jeff McCoy, Carol and Rex Parker, Tina and Craig Peeples, Linda Lee and Bruce Ream, Sharon and Robert Reitsch, Glenda and Craig Shaver, Jan Stenholm-Rathke, Julie (Applequist) and Bob Wallace, Tammy and Bob Washington, Colleen and Brad Wood.

Preface

If you imagine the excitement of the Super Bowl, Stanley Cup, World Series, Olympic Games, and World Cup all rolled into one, you will have some idea of what high school basketball was like in Illinois from the 1930s through the 1950s.

So intense was the interest and so frenzied were the fans that the term "March Madness" was coined in 1939 by Illinois High School Association (IHSA) Assistant Manager H. V. Porter to describe state basketball tournament hysteria. Coincidentally, the team that won the championship that year was Rockford High School, coached by Jim Laude. The following year Rockford High was replaced by two schools, one on each side of the river dividing the city into east and west. Those schools clashed in passionate crosstown competition rivaling the intensity of the state tournament itself.

What follows is the story of how one of those schools, the West High Warriors, went on to win back-to-back IHSA championships in 1955 and 1956, earning the title "the comeback kids" and blazing a trail for ethnic and racial unity in the process.

Warriors Forever is written in part by the 10 year old child in me who was caught up in the state's basketball mania and in part by the grown-up journalist in me who looked behind the scenes and saw the human drama that unfolded before, during, and after those championship seasons.

What emerged after countless hours of interviews and research is far more than just another rah-rah sports story. It is the story of what is best in us and what is worst in us in Everycity, USA, a story for all the seasons of our lives. — John Gile

Warriors Forever

Contents

Tickets to see the Warriors play were a precious and rare commodity. Fans stood in ticket lines for hours, even when there was little hope of getting one. Gymnasiums were packed to the rafters for Warrior games, home and away, during the regular season and at tournament time.

Standing room only

Tickets to West High School basketball games were prized like gold. Players recalled a trick used by alderman Ben Schleicher, later mayor of Rockford, to get his twin brother, Frank, into a game. Ben, a season ticket holder, smeared mud all over his hands before entering and told the ticket attendant at a gym entrance, "Wouldn't you know it, I had a flat tire out there." He asked for a pass so he could go out and wash his hands after using his coat to save a seat for himself in the stands. He received the pass, went in, placed his coat on the bleachers to save his place, then left with the pass and gave it to his brother who was waiting outside. While Ben was in the men's room washing his hands, his brother used the pass to get in through a different entrance. When Ben returned and brandished his clean hands, the attendant waved him in past other ticket holders waiting to enter. That's how desperate fans were to get inside and see the games.

SHAKE. RATTLE. N' ROLL 'EM WEST

Basketball was king in mid-twentieth century America, and high school gymnasiums were the place to be. The games were the centerpiece of weekend social calendars.

The Only Game In Town

In the mid-1950's, fewer than half of the homes in America had a TV. About a third of the homes had no phone. The minimum wage was 75 cents per hour and the average annual salary was about $4,500. New cars cost about $1,900, average new homes about $11,000, and rent was $75 to $85 a month. Gasoline sold for a little more than 20 cents a gallon, bread about 18 cents a loaf, milk about 92 cents a gallon, and postage stamps three cents.

World War II was fresh on everyone's mind and the Korean conflict had ended in an uneasy armistice less than two years earlier. The Cold War was creating so much anxiety that families built bomb shelters in their back yards. Children were taught how to duck under their desks during air raid drills at schools, and the wail of air raid sirens periodically reminded everyone of nuclear peril.

But on Friday and Saturday nights from November through March in cities throughout Illinois, the only thing that mattered was high school basketball. Those lucky enough to have tickets to their local schools' games prepped for what everyone recognized was the social event of the week. Men donned jacket and tie, and women dressed up as if they were going to a dinner-dance. Those without tickets turned on their radios for

3

complete coverage of the action. Wherever friends gathered before or after the game that evening and throughout the next week, their teams' performance and prospects for the next games were the topics of conversation.

In Rockford, Illinois, football-player-turned-basketball-coach Alex Saudargas and a group of boys with extraordinary athletic prowess prepared to enter that world and create a sensation anyone who witnessed it would never forget.

Rockford is located at the top center of Illinois, 18 miles from the Wisconsin border to the north, 85 miles from Chicago to the east, and 90 miles from the Mississippi River to the west. The city prospered as a furniture-maker in the late 1800s and early 1900s, then became a manufacturing power during and after the Second World War. Natural advantages undergird Rockford's perennial resilience and adaptability through changing times: ample water and energy resources; easy access to world markets through air, rail, and interstate highways; a strong labor force bolstered by a regional network of higher education; and a robust cultural life enhanced by surrounding bucolic beauty and world-class attractions.

Sports have always played a major role in the city's community life. In the 1800s, Rockford became one of the first cities in America to have a professional baseball team, the Forest City Nine, featuring sports legend A.G. Spalding and playing against early versions of major league teams from Cincinnati to New York. Spalding was inducted into baseball's Hall of Fame in 1939, the same year Rockford High School prevailed during March Madness. Today Spalding's name is recognized worldwide. It is emblazoned on sports gear used by amateur and professional athletes, including the official National Basketball Association (NBA) and Women's NBA basketballs which are produced by the company Spalding co-founded with his brother.

Even wartime found sports thriving in Rockford. During World War II, thousands of soldiers were inducted and trained at Camp Grant, now the site of the city's international airport. Drafted athletes from around the country played for Camp Grant football teams while preparing for war duty. Like West High later, Rockford's Camp Grant teams were known as the Warriors. Camp Grant's 1943 team, led by prewar Notre

Dame fullback Corwinn Clatt, got off to a good start, drubbing the University of Illinois 23 to 0 and defeating the University of Wisconsin 10 to 7. Colgate University's prewar football captain Bob Orlando sealed the Camp Grant victory over Wisconsin with a 30-yard field goal in the last five seconds. Between those victories, about 11,000 sports fans in Rockford witnessed future NFL Hall-of-Famer Elroy "Crazylegs" Hirsch

leading the University of Michigan to a 26 to 0 rout of Rockford's eleven. Hirsch scored two touchdowns, including his runback of the opening kickoff, and set up another Michigan touchdown with a pass interception.

Elroy "Crazylegs" Hirsch led the Michigan Wolverines to victory over Rockford's Camp Grant Warriors.

War years brought still more baseball fame to the city. Rockford's Beyer Stadium was home to the Rockford Peaches of the All-American Girls Professional Baseball League formed by Chicago Cubs' owner P.K. Wrigley and other major league team owners. The Rockford Peaches won four league championships and were memorialized in "A League of Their Own," an award-winning film achieving commercial success in both the United States and abroad.

Rockford also has contributed to player development for Major League Baseball and for the National Hockey League. The Montreal Expos and the Chicago Cubs fielded minor league teams in Rockford and the Chicago Blackhawks formed a player development affiliation with the Rockford IceHogs of the American Hockey League. More than a dozen former IceHogs put sticks on the ice with Blackhawk teams capturing Stanley Cup championships for Chicago.

But getting tickets to see professional athletes perform in Rockford was never as difficult as getting tickets to see high school basketball games. West High standout Rod Coffman, starting guard for the 1955 champions, described mob scenes he encountered at the team's home games. "When I tried to walk in through the front door before the sophomore games started, there would be hundreds of people trying to get in. Visiting teams were given tickets and would always turn back to the school any that weren't used. So there would be a few tickets available, 40 or 50 at the most, but there would be about 500 people standing there trying to buy them. It was just an exciting time."

That excitement reached fever pitch when Rockford's East and West High Schools clashed. "There is something about an East-West game that all but defies description," local sportswriter Jim Johnston, wrote. "The intensity of feeling, the singleness of purpose, and the constant roar of frenzy from the stands set this spectacle apart from anything else on the sports calendar. It happens at least twice a year, but its greatness never seems to diminish."

What doesn't kill you makes you stronger

Quiet defiance and calm courage in the face of discrimination or unfairness were lifelong traits of West High Coach Alex Saudargas — and the spirit of West High from its inception.

"We came from the crumbling Rockford Central High School, the first graduating class from West High in 1941, kids of the Depression who graduated to war the following December." — Lucy Abramsom Sands, '41.

"West is a melting pot of students from different races, creeds, nationalities, and incomes. Each contributes to give West an identity like no other high school."
—Josephine Licari, '89

ROCKFORD MORNING

SECTION 2   ROCKFORD, ILLINOIS, SUNDAY, AUGUST 14, 1938   PAGE THIRTEEN

Here Is Artist's Sketch Of Proposed West Senior High School

From the KKK to the WPA

West High School was built as part of President Franklin Delano Roosevelt's job-creating Works Progress Administration (WPA) program spawned by the Great Depression. Planning began in 1938, funding was provided in 1939, and construction was completed in 1940. Famed architect Jesse Barloga, designer of more than 400 architectural projects in the Midwest and a member of the World War II team that engineered the B-29 bomber, was a consulting architect for the school's design and construction.

Because West High neighborhoods always have been multicultural and multiracial, West was a rainbow school decades before Archbishop Desmond Tutu coined the term to describe South Africa's racially diverse alliance formed under President Nelson Mandela in 1994.

As with so many industrial cities in the North, cultural and racial diversity did not come easily to Rockford. Ironically, West High was located in the city's northwest quadrant on the southwest corner of North Rockton Avenue and Custer Street, kitty-corner from the former site of an entertainment venue called Driving Park. Just a few years before West was built, Driving Park was the site of the Clyde Beatty Carnival, the Ringling Brothers Barnum and Bailey Circus — and Ku Klux Klan rallies. Local Ku

Klux Klan bigotry and violence were directed against all of the city's ethnic, racial, and religious minorities.

Byron Anderson, a Rockford businessman who lived near Driving Park in his childhood and whose family was Roman Catholic, recalled being terrified by hooded Klansmen's torchlight parades in his neighborhood. "We lived on Huffman Boulevard along the east border of Driving Park. The KKK would parade north up Huffman Boulevard past our house, turn left at Bell Avenue, then turn left into Driving Park through the stone archway entrance on Bell. I would run and hide under my bed."

KKK cross burnings at Driving Park and at the homes of minorities who struggled against Klan rule were part of the Rockford landscape for decades. Isabel Culhane, a reporter for one of Rockford's daily newspapers in the 1960s, said her father-in-law, T. H. Culhane, an Irish Catholic physician who was active in public affairs, felt Klan wrath when he fought a school board faction that opposed allowing Catholic women to teach in the public schools. She said that Klansmen burned a cross at Dr. Culhane's home, 1003 North Church Street, but he stood his ground and, with the support of Sarah Thomas, a non-Catholic and a teacher, overcame the bigoted opposition.

Both Alex Saudargas, the man destined to lead the West High Warriors to eminence in Illinois sports, and his future wife Alice encountered discrimination in their youth and in later years. Coach Saudargas was the son of Lithuanian immigrants who came to America to get away from Russian occupation of their homeland. The family encountered caste makers in Rockford who had codified their bigotry with restrictive covenants prohibiting sales of land and homes to Blacks, Jews, Irish, Italians, Lithuanians, Asians, and just about anyone else who fell outside their own narrow, ethno-racial clique.

Alice was the daughter of Norwegian immigrants who met and were married in Chicago, then settled on farmland near Fairdale, a farming community about 20 miles southeast of Rockford. Her family's Norwegian language and culture were not welcomed readily in the predominantly English Fairdale, and Alice recalled suffering abuse that included a severe beating by her English classmates in a school cloakroom.

Their firsthand experiences with discrimination imbued both Alice and Coach Saudargas with heightened sympathy for victims of bigotry and unfair treatment all their lives. "From the beginning of his teaching and coaching career, my husband was sensitive to and fought against all forms of discrimination," said Alice, his wife of 60 years. "There were some people, some vocal people, who didn't want to have black players on the court. We used to get telephone calls about it. I would get the phone calls asking for my husband. They would be terribly abusive.

"If a call came in when I was out, sometimes our children would answer. I remember coming home from a game one night in particular. We had a babysitter for the younger children so the older children could go to the game. When I came home, our little girl, Shirley, said, 'This woman called and she was screaming on the phone about my daddy over there with all those . . .' And she went on and on and on. Of course, our little girl didn't know what it was all about, but the caller was really rude and Shirley was scared.

"Redlining was common then, too. Banks would partition the city so black families couldn't get bank loans for homes in certain areas. And there were real estate people who would show black families homes for sale only in southwest Rockford.

"Alex encountered more discrimination in his work outside of school, too," she said. "School teachers were not paid much in those days, so he took a job selling pots and pans door to door to supplement our income. He was told specifically that he could not sell any pots and pans to black girls or black families. He went ahead and did it anyway, then blurred and muddied the race designation on the contract."

West High's varsity football and sophomore basketball coach Don Kriechbaum said the Warriors sometimes encountered discrimination on trips to games at other schools. "On one trip, we took the players into a restaurant and were ready to order when we were told that the black players would have to eat in the kitchen. Alex and the rest of us coaches ordered everybody up and herded them out of the restaurant."

Coach Kriechbaum said, "There were some places farther south where we had to be especially watchful. I remember we had to tell the kids, 'When you get off the bus, you stay with the team. You don't ever go out there alone' because there were some people in those cities who were racists. We made sure players got off the bus and went right into the gym."

Coach Saudargas extended his protection for players to their educations, also, Alice said. "He always arranged for any of the players, white or black, who were having problems academically to have tutors. He emphasized education and reminded players that education came first, sports second.

"Rockford industry, like companies in cities across the nation's manufacturing belt, recruited heavily to lure cheap labor from the South, but the school system made no effort to accommodate the needs of the children who came north with their parents. Some students who arrived in Rockford from the South, especially black students, couldn't read because they came from areas that didn't have the kinds of classes we had up here in kindergarten, first grade, and so forth. They were not able to do the work at the elementary level, so the district just labeled them 'mentally handicapped' and tossed them into special education classes."

Coach Kriechbaum said the teacher and parent community at West High worked to overcome that. "We had a strong bond of togetherness at West High, and we were colorblind," he said. "Teachers would tell the coaches if any players were weak or in trouble in any of their classes or whatever, and we would see that the students received help. News traveled around and everybody was looking out for everybody. Even the school nurse would work with players. If the nurse knew that players were injured in the last game, she would check on them to see how they were doing. I know that some of the varsity parents were looking out for any of the kids who were coming from difficult situations, too. That all goes along with success, you know. That's gotta happen. When players arrived at West High, it was like they were coming into another family."

A formula for success

Alice Saudargas, the one who knew Coach Saudargas best, said there were three reasons for her husband's success: "He was never judgmental. He had a knack for drawing people out. And he never took credit for anything. He went out of his way to find ways to make others the star."

Swish! Coach Saudargas scores for his homeroom students.

Marching to a Different Drummer

When Alex Saudargas became head basketball coach for the West High School Warriors, he was overshadowed by Rockford's decades-long winning tradition and by the reigning East High Coach James Laude.

Rockford was a basketball powerhouse even before the inception of state tournaments in 1908. Rockford High School refused to participate in that first tournament, an invitational tournament hosted by the Oak Park YMCA, because the consensus of the day's major media sportswriters and prevailing popular opinion had deemed Rockford "champions of the state" by acclamation. No one in Rockford saw any reason to defend their unofficial title in the Oak Park tournament. That changed in 1910, and Rockford won the IHSA State Basketball Championship at Peoria in 1911 under coach Ralph Vennum. Rockford defeated Mount Carroll for the championship that year 60 to 15. That 45 point victory margin set a tournament championship game record that was never matched or topped in subsequent years.

Rockford reached the state tournament finals again under coach Frank Winters in 1916, 1918, 1919, and 1920. Winters' team won the championship in 1919, but failed to make the final four the other three years.

Under coach E. U. McDonald, Rockford won second place in 1921, but failed to the make the final four during downstate tournament action in 1922 and 1923.

When Coach Laude took over as head basketball coach at Rockford, he led the 1927, 1935, and 1938 teams into the state tournaments, but never made it to the final four until his championship season in 1939.

While the exploits of Coach Laude and his basketball teams were featured in headlines, Saudargas was playing football for undefeated Rockford High School teams, winning All-State honors his senior year. He was awarded a football scholarship to Northern Illinois State Teachers College, now Northern Illinois University (NIU), in DeKalb, and earned seven letters there, three in wrestling and four in football. He played guard in every game for Northern all four years and received All-Conference Second Team honors his senior year.

Alice said he never tried out for basketball because he determined his physique and ability were more suited for football and wrestling, but he became interested in the sport and began studying the dynamics of basketball at games he saw in Northern's gymnasium. After completing undergraduate work, he went on to Champaign-Urbana where he earned a Masters Degree in administration from the University of Illinois.

When Saudargas returned to Rockford after completing his Masters Degree work, the old Rockford High School had been closed and replaced by the new East and West High Schools. Laude was named coach at East High and took his teams to state tournaments in 1945, 1946, 1947, and 1948, finishing fourth in 1946 and second in 1948, but never bringing home the championship trophy for East High. West played under three different coaches those years and never was able to be competitive in the conference or in crosstown clashes, losing seven straight games to East High in 1940 through 1943, winning one game, then losing eight straight from 1944 through 1948.

Saudargas was assigned to his first coaching and teaching position at Morris Kennedy School in Rockford. His team there won 19 games and lost none. From Morris Kennedy, he moved on to become school superintendent at Seward, a grade and high school in a rural area about 20 miles west of Rockford. He coached the first winning basketball team in Seward's history with a record of 25 wins and two losses and won the county championship. In 1943 he returned to Rockford and coached basketball at Washington Junior High School, leading his team there to 23 wins with no losses. After Washington, he moved to East High School for one year as a teacher, sophomore football and basketball coach, and head track coach. His next position was as teacher and head basketball coach at Roosevelt Junior High School where he produced another city champion before being named head basketball coach at West High in 1947.

When Saudargas arrived at West to take over the basketball program, he brought with him a coaching style radically different from the methods used by East High's popular and boisterous Coach Laude. While Laude stormed up and down the floor yelling at his players and at the referees, Saudargas sat in calm reserve and never raised his voice. It was a style that became a Saudargas trademark in subsequent years, a style he developed deliberately and explained to his oldest son, Alex, years later.

"When one of his players was the victim of a bad call by the referees or if the ball went out of bounds after obviously being touched by the other team but the referees failed to call it that way, he just ignored it," Alex said. "One day he told me why he did that.

"He said, 'In the thrill of the game, good things are going to happen and bad things are going to happen, but at the end of the game, it's only the score that matters. If you're going to be on top, if you're going to win, you can't afford to waste your energy complaining about bad things that happen. If you do, you let two more bad things happen: first, you waste your energy, you deplete your energy on something you can't do anything about anyway, something you can't control; second, when you complain about bad things that happen, you lose your focus, you allow yourself to be distracted from your goal and from the things you can control.' That was his philosophy: focus on your goal and on doing your best at what you can control. That is what he taught his players and what he demonstrated for them by his own example."

Others, including a younger son Richard Saudargas, Ph.D., a professor of psychology at the University of Tennessee in Knoxville, recalled his father applying that principle at practice sessions. "When you watched and listened to how he worked with people, you could see that he was a natural teacher," Richard said. "He didn't believe in criticizing or berating his players, and he couldn't understand why other coaches did that. No one has ever been criticized into success.

"At practice sessions, he would show the players how to run the plays, but if something went wrong, he would have them stop and start to do it all over again from the beginning. He would walk them through on how to do it correctly, using repetition, backing up and starting over again. That's a solid psychological principle, backing up to the beginning and going all through the entire steps rather than just working on pieces. He was a natural teacher, a natural psychologist."

It wasn't long before his teaching and coaching techniques began paying off in victories for Saudargas' Warriors. During his first five years at West, his Warriors won two regional championships, one in 1949 and another in 1952. His 1949 team went on to the state tournament, but didn't make the final four that year.

As Saudargas was sharpening his coaching skills and achieving goals at West, future Warriors were sharpening their basketball skills wherever they could find a hoop in West High neighborhoods.

Pursuing the dream

"Even back in the sixth, seventh, and eighth grades, all we wanted to do was make the basketball team when we got to high school." Dave McClelland, a 1955 Warrior reserve, said. "That was our dream. Saturday mornings, Saturday afternoons, Sunday afternoons, after school every day, whenever we were free, we were outside shooting baskets in the alley or wherever we could play. We got a basket and put it up on the garage. In winter we'd shovel snow off the driveway so we could shoot baskets even though our hands got cold doing it. We knew about all the players on the West High teams because we read about them and saw their pictures in the newspapers. We didn't get to see them play because tickets were in such demand that it was impossible in those years for us to actually see the real game, but we would listen on the radio. We couldn't go to the barbershop or any place like that without hearing people talk about the players and the coaches and the games."

Don Grabow, 52, shared every West-Side athlete's passion for becoming one of Coach Saudargas' Warriors. Huddled with Grabow and Coach Saudargas are Rod Coffman and Rex Parker, 43.

For Love of the Game

Don Grabow was a key player on the 1955 championship team, voted Best Sixth Man on any of the tournament teams by Illinois sportswriters covering the action. Grabow chronicled his own story in a journal, but he was also telling the story of countless other aspiring Warriors growing up in West High neighborhoods.

"When we lived on Loomis Street in South Rockford," he wrote, "there was an alley next to our house and a garage in the alley. We took a bushel basket, cut the bottom out of it, and nailed it to the garage. The alley was made up of cinders, so we would bloody our hands and knees as we played, but we would play for hours anyway.

"Sometimes I would take long walks, about seven miles, to the north side of town to shoot baskets at the asphalt court on the Roosevelt Junior High School playground. Afterwards I would walk around the neighborhoods just hoping to see one of the local sports stars who were my heroes: Bob Griggas, Ray Paul, Bob Richards, Kenny Kohler, Bob Reitsch, guys who were a few years ahead of me in school.

"When my parents moved to Custer Avenue only three blocks from West High, I would walk up and practice or play in pickup games on the outdoor courts there all day. I would practice left hand hook shots, right hand hook shots, left hand jump shots, right hand jump shots, left hand layups, right hand layups, reverse layups, left and right. I did them all for hour after hour, day after day. I shot so many free throws I could make them in my sleep or with a blindfold on. I had one dream and one dream only: to play for the Warriors. Two-hundred guys showed up for tryouts, but only 12 were going to make it."

Rex Parker, a starting guard on the 1955 championship team, got started playing basketball the same way. "When we lived in the far west end of Rockford, my dad put up a hoop and backboard on a telephone pole in the back yard," he said. "Then he graveled the area for us to use as a basketball court. We would shovel snow off it in the wintertime and keep our gloves on to play."

Other future Warriors were on the same path as Grabow and Parker. Bobby Washington, a reserve on the 1955 championship team and a starting guard in 1956, recalled a heavily used basketball hoop behind Barbour School in South Rockford. "Even in the winter," he said, "we would clear snow to shoot baskets. That's how enthusiastic we were about wanting to become really good players."

"What we all had in common was a strong work ethic. We were lower middle class, even the Roosevelt Junior High School kids who joined us at West. Some of them may have had a little more privilege than others, maybe a little more money, but basically we all knew you had to earn what you got, that nobody was going to give you anything. Most of our parents had very little formal education and had to work very hard, but they valued education for us. They taught us right from wrong, core values that we learned as kids growing up. So we learned to compete and expected to compete."

More future Warrior standouts joined Washington at the basketball hoop behind Barbour School, including Nolden Gentry, a starter and star on both the 1955 and 1956 championship teams and later a starter and star at the University of Iowa. "In my youth, every time I got near a basketball, I practiced, practiced, and then practiced some more," Gentry said. "Inside, I shot at a clothes basket on a chair in our basement. That effort supported my focus: to be the best basketball player that I could be."

"It wasn't long before organized programs were established," Washington said, "Melwood Davis, the athletic director at Booker Washington Community Center in our neighborhood, is the one who got us organized and playing in the Jaycee League at the Boys Club downtown. Because the Center couldn't afford uniforms, we went door to door selling raffle tickets and earned enough money to get team shirts, but each of us wore whatever shorts we had at home. The Moose Club and the Elks Club had shiny, new, full uniforms and they beat us. That first year everybody beat us.

"The next year we raised more money and bought complete uniforms. We were getting better that year. Finally we went on to have an undefeated season, winning the regular season Jaycee League, winning the Holiday Tournament, and finishing with a record of 27 wins and no losses.

That team had a lot of future Warriors: Don Slaughter, a 1955 reserve and 1956 starter; Gentry; Roscoe Burke, a 1956 reserve, Raymond Morgan, a 1955 reserve, and Luther Bedford, a 1955 reserve."

Parker traced his introduction to organized league play back to his years at Lincoln Park Grade School and his coach, Walter Bowland. "Coach Bowland was a big, strong southern boy who was chased out of Georgia by the Ku Klux Klan after talking against the Klan in the school where he taught and coached," Parker said. "He had a lot of integrity, and stood up to the Klan when they pressured him to change his ways. After they burned a cross in his yard, he decided to leave there and moved to Rockford because a sister was living here. He showed respect for everyone and treated everyone the same, and we were expected to follow his example. He was so committed to civil rights that he received a Freedom House Award of Merit in 1949 at Carnegie Hall in New York for his stands against the Klan in Georgia.

Coach Walter Bowland

"We didn't have a gym at the school then," Parker said, "so two or three times a week during basketball season Coach Bowland would pile anywhere from eight to 12 of us kids into his big Packard and take us downtown to the Rockford Boys Club where we practiced.

"That led to our getting involved in the Jaycee League. My dad was in the heating business, and he sponsored our team, the Parker Heat. We played on Saturdays against teams from all over the Rockford and Loves Park area and came to know all their players. At the same time, we had teams in what was called the Winnebago County Grade School League and played against Morris Kennedy, Whig Hill, Rock River, and Durand Farm School as well as against Loves Park grade schools. I played on the Lincoln Park team that was undefeated for three years."

Parker said one of his good friends at Lincoln Park School was his future 1955 Warrior teammate Rod Coffman. "Rod moved to the East Side when he was in the fifth grade, so he ended up playing for Morris Kennedy School and later for Lincoln Junior High School. He was playing for the Morris Kennedy team that ended our three year winning streak. We were competitors, but we were always friends because we had roots back to the second grade. As soon as the game was over, we were friends again.

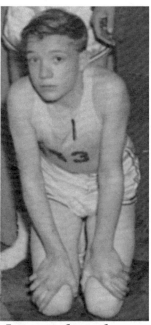

In seventh grade, Rod Coffman was an East-Sider playing for Morris Kennedy School against Rex Parker and other future Warriors.

"About that time, Lincoln Park Grade School added a gym and the Kiwanis Club built the Lincoln Park Boys Club. That opened up a lot of opportunities for many of the kids in the West End. We didn't have to go to the Rockford Boys Club downtown to practice anymore because we had both the grade school gym and the Lincoln Park Boys Club.

"After eighth grade, we had the option of going to either Washington Junior High School in South Rockford or to Roosevelt Junior High in the North End. Most of us chose Roosevelt because it was a little closer. When I got to Roosevelt, I met other future Warrior championship teammates who were already there: Fred Boshela,

Don Grabow, Johnny Wessels, Sam Black, Tom Olson, Dave McClelland, and Sam Patton. We meshed and started playing ball together, and that was really when we started thinking that maybe we could achieve something someday.

"At the same time, 1955 Warrior starter Gentry and 1955 Warrior reserves Washington, Burke, Bedford, Morgan, and Joe DiGiovanni went to Washington Junior High. They were very competitive and very good. The West Side junior high schools, Roosevelt and Washington, and an East Side junior high, Lincoln, played against each other and against the freshman teams from Harlem High School in Loves Park and schools from Beloit, WI, and Freeport. At Washington and at Roosevelt, our coaches acquainted players with the kind of style that Coach Saudargas was using at West, so we started playing a little bit more serious ball, acquiring new skills, and raising our level of playing."

Coffman said there was so much interest in basketball, so many fans wanting to know what players they could look forward to seeing in the years ahead, that media coverage of promising players started at the grade school level. "They always had blurbs in the paper about our games," he said. "All the players who ended up playing at West — Gentry, Parker, Washington, Wessels, Boshela, Grabow, me — our names were in the paper from grade school on up. Fan interest was building from the time we were in elementary school all the way through junior high and into high school."

But player interest was building even more, Grabow noted in his journal. "All the good athletes from both Washington and Roosevelt would be coming to West. Knowing that drew us together in a sense of companionship and competitiveness. Guys who once were 'enemies' were now becoming friends and teammates. We played basketball every day and developed a winning attitude. We would go to different parks and play against guys from different parts of the city, choosing sides and playing against each other. We became so good we would know where and what our teammates were going to do without even looking."

But someone else was looking: Coach Saudargas. "Almost every day of the summer he would go around town and watch the kids play pickup basketball," Alice said. "He really enjoyed that. He had a knack for spotting players. He watched for speed, agility, and an eye so they could shoot. And he always looked for smart kids, kids who could listen and learn. He said you have to have smart kids because you can't be out there on the floor telling them what to do every minute of the game. That's what you do in practice. Then, in game situations, they can figure out for themselves what's the right thing to do."

Planting a vision

"The first time I had a chance to meet Alex Saudargas," Nolden Gentry said, "was after our seventh grade year in the Rockford Boys Club when we went undefeated. Coach Saudargas came to the All Sports Banquet at Booker Washington Center and gave a great speech." Bobby Washington remembered that speech, too, and said it made a deep impression on him. "He told us that we played like champions and, if we worked hard and stayed together, we could be state champions. We never thought about that before. He planted that vision and I never forgot it. It increased my interest in basketball and made me want to be better. He said we would be better if we used both hands, learned to shoot with our left hand as well as our right hand. He said it and we believed it. Everything he said that night came true."

Future Warrior standouts were groomed for greatness by Coach Don Larson at Washington Junior High School. Larson, later head football coach at Illinois Wesleyan University in Bloomington, is flanked by, left to right, Roscoe Burke, Bobby Washington, Nolden Gentry, Ray Morgan, and Luther Bedford. After graduating from West High, Morgan and Bedford played football for Larson at Illinois Wesleyan.

The Telltale Tourney

Rex Parker said he and some of his Warrior teammates who entered West High in the fall of 1952 started thinking about winning the state tournament when Freeport, with Carl Cain and McKinley "Deacon" Davis, won the IHSA crown in 1951. "Everybody admired that group. They were big and they were powerful and they won the whole state tournament. We thought, 'Hey, if somebody down the road can do it, why can't we?'"

More fuel was added to the state championship fire the following year when tiny Hebron, with a population of 650 and a high school enrollment of 98, won the state tournament in a David versus Goliath battle against the team from Quincy, a city of 44,000. Hebron, about 40 miles east of Rockford, played its home games on the cramped confines of an old auditorium stage and became the smallest school ever to win the single class Boys Basketball Championship.

"But I think the real event that got us started thinking seriously about state championships happened when we were sophomores," Parker said. "We were coached by Don Kriechbaum and Jim Pence. We tied with

East High for second place in the conference and then played in Belvidere's tournament at the end of the season.

"Belvidere had hosted for many years a 32 team frosh-soph basketball tournament at their community center, and it had become a standing tradition that the sophomore team that won the Belvidere tournament would reach the state tournament their senior year. The teams didn't necessarily win the state tournaments, but the tradition was that the Belvidere winner would be in the state tournament as seniors.

"That was a big kicker for us because we did win that as a sophomore team in 1953. We had a strong team, with players who had come over from both Roosevelt Junior High and Washington Junior High, many of whom would play on the 1955 championship team: Don Grabow, Fred Boshela, Luther Bedford, Tom Olson, Rease Binger, Ray Morgan, and me. We ended up with a record of 18 wins and two losses that year, including the tournament victories. But winning the tournament was very meaningful for us."

Bobby Washington said the same thing happened the next year, when he and others from the Roosevelt and Washington Junior High teams entered West. "Gentry played on the varsity, but the sophomore team had players who later played on the championship teams: Tom Blake, Johnny Wessels, Joe DiGiovanni, Sam Patton, Roscoe Burke, and me. We finished with 17 wins, one loss, and were first in the Big Eight Conference. Everything that was happening reinforced the championship vision."

Coach Kriechbaum said, "Except for Gentry, who was called up to the varsity, that whole sophomore group in 1954 was more or less kept together during the regular season. When the Belvidere tournament came around, though, Gentry came to me and said he wanted to be with the team one time. He said, 'In your next game, may I come and dress and sit on the bench? I don't care if I don't play, but I want to be on that team with them.' That's how close together those guys were.

"I asked Alex and got permission for him to dress with his sophomore teammates for one game, but I also had an agreement with Gentry that I wasn't going to take any players out just to put him into the game. I wasn't going to be playing him instead of my regulars. Well, it happened that we got a lead and it was easy to put him in for the last few minutes of a quarter. Gentry was great to deal with."

"Gentry," Coach Saudargas told a Chicago audience, "is the type of player every coach dreams about. He has the height — he is slightly taller than 6'6" in stocking feet. He is agile. He is aggressive. He can score. He can rebound. And above all, he is the perfect team player.

"Gentry scores less than he could because he is the one who constantly seeks to set up the others. He has plenty of fine shots, is one of the best free throw artists in the area, and can fake and feed with the best. And on tip-ins, his height and agility are tops.

"Defensively, Gentry is even more of a standout. His long arms and lightning quick hands block shots which normally would be easy. He seems to be everywhere at once and is always trouble to the opposition.

"Gentry is the kid you can count on every time in the clutch. He has proven outstanding ability and poise in all the important phases of

Warrior forward Nolden Gentry

the game: consistency, courage, and temperament, especially when the going is tough; intelligence and receptiveness to coaching; and character to be a gentleman on and off the playing court."

Coach Saudagas' oldest son Alex said, "I always looked up to Gentry because he had such a great presence, a commanding type of presence. When he walked into the room, he was one of those guys that you just stopped to look at. His presence just took over the room. I think he got that demeanor from his Mom and Dad. They were terrific people, too, a great family. He was smart and fun to be around, playful and yet he was so kind and dedicated. You could tell this guy had already developed a purpose in life, even then.

"My brother Richard and I were watching practice one afternoon and Richard asked, 'Who do you think the best player is?' I said, 'I don't know who the best player is, but I know who the best guy is – Nolden Gentry.' He was always so nice to me. Sometimes I'd show up at practice and he'd throw balls back and forth and let me shoot a couple baskets. He was always so kind and humble. I remember hearing him talk after games, and he'd give credit to everybody else even when it was he who really made the difference."

"In fact," Coach Kriechbaum said, "all the Warriors had that team spirit or they wouldn't have been on the team. We didn't have any prima donnas. It was the team first and the individual second."

It's a team game

Coach Saudargas' oldest son Alex said his father made sure all the players understood that each of them had an important role to play in the team's success. "I remember times when Dad would gather the team, starters and reserves, and tell them, 'Basketball is a team game, and every one of you is making an important contribution, whether it's here at practice or on the court during the game. That's what makes each one of you special. Never forget that.'"

*Not every player was in the headlines every week, but every Warrior
contributed to West High's success day in and day out, week in and
week out at grueling practices, sharpening the skills of the starters as
well as their own, and preparing to fill in whenever Coach Saudargas
called on them. The 1955 state champion Warriors are, front row, left
to right: Coach Saudargas, Robert "Bobby" Washington, Luther
Bedford, Rex Parker, Ray Morgan, and Rease Binger. Second row:
Manager Doug Reed, Dave McClelland, Jeff McCoy, Sam Black, Sam
Patton, Manager Bruce Ream. Back row, inset, Rod Coffman, absent
the day the photo was taken; Tom Olson, Joe DiGiovanni, Fred
Boshela, Nolden Gentry, Johnny Wessels, and Don Slaughter.*

Unsung Heroes

Warrior reserves were a star-studded squad of gifted athletes who were standouts earlier on junior high, sophomore, and junior varsity championship teams and whose names were widely recognized around Rockford for their athletic achievements: Don Grabow, Bob Washington, Luther Bedford, Sam Black, Dave McClelland, Tommy Olson, Joe DiGiovanni, Jeff McCoy, Roscoe Burke, Sam Patton, Ray Morgan, and Rease Binger. The bench was so packed with talent that it was common knowledge most Warrior reserves would be starters on other teams. Starting guard Rex Parker said, "Our varsity team my senior year had at least ten or twelve players who were all pretty close in their level of ability and competitiveness. Any one of those ten or twelve would have been outstanding players at other schools around the state or around the country."

So talented were the '54-'55 West High reserves that one writer quipped to Coach Saudargas, "You take the starters to the state tournament and I'll take the bench. Together we'll win both first place and second place."

Some of the players would go on to become well known throughout the state of Illinois for their timely contributions to Warriors' championship campaigns. Some would become known later for their achievements on their college football, basketball, and baseball teams,

Others would follow in Coach Saudargas' footsteps after their Warrior championship seasons and be part of the Saudargas legacy by becoming well known coaches themselves. Rease Binger went on to play basketball for Northwestern University and later coached Decatur High School in mid-state Illinois to two Regional basketball titles. Luther Bedford became a four-year varsity starter in football at Illinois Wesleyan University, making all-conference three of his four years and voted Most Valuable Player his senior year.

Bedford went on to Chicago's Marshall High School, coaching football for five years and winning a city championship, coaching baseball for six years, and coaching basketball for 27 years, winning three city championships and leading his teams to state tournaments four times. He topped off his Warrior-spawned career by being elected to the Illinois Basketball Coaches' Hall of Fame, the Chicago Public League Basketball Coaches' Hall of Fame, and by being featured in two films, *Hoop Dreams* in 1994 and *Hoop Reality* in 2007.

Like Coach Saudargas at West High, Coach Bedford became known and loved at Marshall for his commitment to and compassion for his students and athletes in every aspect of their lives, not just in high school athletics. Cook County's Board of Commissioners cited his work as "a diligent and dedicated coach, teacher, and mentor of young people" in a proclamation honoring him when he died at age 69. Later the Chicago Public League Coaches' Association All-Star Game was renamed the Luther Bedford Memorial Public League All-Star Game in his honor.

Other reserves went on to manifest the Warrior spirit by scaling the heights in their chosen fields and by providing both example and counseling from their own experiences to help others achieve success in life despite devastating mistakes and setbacks. Such was the nature of the spirited Warrior reserves.

Though Warrior reserves had little time on the court during games and garnered no headlines or fanfare, they came to practice day after day and used their talents to test the mettle of the starters and to sharpen and strengthen the starters' skills. In intrasquad games at practice, Warrior starters often found themselves pitted against players whose skills and competitive spirit matched or exceeded those of opponents they met during the season or in tournament play.

Coach Saudargas' oldest son Alex said, "I remember watching intrasquad games when the reserves would get the best of the starters. Dad enjoyed having his second team practicing at that level and doing so well. Bobby Washington, for example, wasn't a starter in the '55 championship season, but he would do some amazing things at practice along with the rest of the reserves."

Senior Dave McClelland, cited in preseason media reports as a 6'5" junior varsity star "who will be a ready assistant at forward and center" for the Warriors' varsity in the new season, attested to both the talent pool and the intensity of the vigorous intrasquad games, one of which put him in the hospital. "Our junior varsity team beat East High by 44 points," McClelland said. "The next year, those East High junior varsity players moved up to become varsity starters at East. At the same time, our West High junior varsity regulars moved up to become second and third team Warriors. We had four returning varsity starters from the previous year joined by John Wessels, a junior classmate of starting forward Nolden Gentry, both of whom were a year behind us in school."

He said practices were intense all season. "School was over at three-thirty and we practiced until five-thirty or six o'clock. If the gym was being used by another team after school, we went home, did our homework and so forth, then came back at six o'clock and practiced till eight or eight-thirty. We would warm up with a kind of shoot-around and then, when practice actually started, we drilled on fundamentals. We never lost sight of fundamentals. There were lay-ups, jump shots from the free throw line, from the back of the circle, one-on-one drills, and two-on-one, and things like that. We never put those aside no matter how far into the season we were.

"When we had one-on-one drills, we really went at it. We didn't just go through the motions. We did it like it was game time. Then we would run through the plays with no defense on the court, just to learn how to run the plays, learning what the options were for this or that situation."

Rease Binger remembered the intense practices and drills. "My job in practice, every practice, was playing one on one with Fred Boshela, the starting forward," he said. "Coach Saudargas put me against Fred because I was small and quick and Fred had to learn to protect the ball from being stolen. It wasn't for me that Coach Saudargas was doing it. It was for Fred. So every day we spent 10 or 15 minutes one on one. It helped Fred during the games and, as it turned out, it helped me later when I went on to play ball at Northwestern. I didn't think what I was doing was very important, but I did enjoy being there. We all felt a part of the team, and all of us were contributing in the best way we could."

McClelland said the intrasquad games would come at the end of practice, after all the drills and running through plays. The intensity of the competition landed him in the hospital a week before the first game of the season. "One morning I woke up on the third floor of Rockford Memorial Hospital just north of the school," he said. "I didn't have a clue how I got there. It was kinda predawn, kinda foggy, overcast, and I said to myself, 'Hey there's the school down there. I'm in the hospital. What am I doing here? Nothing's broken, I don't think we got into an auto accident.'

"Later I was told I took an elbow to the head during our intrasquad game and then went head first into the floor. I don't remember what happened next, but my teammates said I was told to go sit on the sidelines, then get dressed to go home. The school custodian said when I got to the locker room I kept asking, 'What happened? Where am I?' Somehow I guess I got dressed, but when the guys came down from practice I started to go into the shower with them, only I was fully clothed. My teammate Tom Olson gave me and our teammate Sam Black rides back and forth to school, and we rode home with him that night. Sam was dropped off first, so he went right in and called my folks to tell them I was coming home but didn't seem okay to him. I guess my parents agreed because they put me in the car and took me to the hospital where the doctors said I had a concussion and needed to be admitted.

"When the coaches and the principal found out I had a concussion, they told me not to even bother coming to practice till after Christmas, so I lost several weeks. They may have been overreacting and were being a little overcautious. It looked as though I wouldn't be able to come back till

January, but I finally was able to dress for games and see a little action in the holiday tournament."

McClelland said another trait the Warriors had in common was a strong work ethic. "I have vivid memories of Fred Boshela, for example, going back to the sixth grade. I had an evening paper route, the Rockford Register Republic, and part of the route was up the Church Street hill where the Boshela family lived. Even at that age, I picked up that his home life was not ideal and he had to work hard and fend for himself."

"In junior high and high school, he was a regular pinsetter at Simon's Recreation, a bowling alley on North Main Street not far from where many of us lived. That was before we had mechanical pinsetters, and it was very rough work. Any time I ever went there, on weekday nights, Saturday afternoons, or Sunday afternoons, he was working in back with the bowling pins. That was how he earned the money he needed for high school. I always had a special admiration for Fred because of what I saw on my paper route and from seeing him work the way he did.

"Most of us had jobs in high school," McClelland said. "Local business owners were fans of school teams, so they would let us fit our work schedules around school and basketball practice. When I got too old for paper routes and caddying at Rockford Country Club, I went in to Auburn Street Hardware near my home and asked for a job. The owner said, 'Yeah, I'll hire you for fifty cents an hour, but you won't be worth anything to me for at least three months while you learn the business.' He was right. I would go to the store after school and work for about an hour and a half. The owner knew I was a basketball player, so he told me to come in Saturday mornings and leave at three o'clock if we had a game. Other players had the same kind of support at their jobs. Almost all of us were accustomed to working and earning our own money.

"Instilling the work ethic in players was one of the things my husband did very well," Alice Saudargas said, "and most of their families, did, too. My husband always made sure the players took responsibility for themselves and for the decisions they made. They were responsible for getting to class on time and to practice on time and to the bus taking them to road games on time. They were responsible for taking care of their uniforms. Players would sometimes try to blame somebody else for their problems and say, 'It's not my fault,' or 'He made me do it.' But that never worked with my husband. Teaching his players to take responsibility for their actions and for their team was part of his program. That work ethic was something he instilled and demanded at practice, at games, in the classroom, on the road, as a quality of character that went through everything all the time."

Tests of character — on and off the court — lay ahead for the Warriors and for both Alex and Alice.

More than a coach

"Coach Saudargas changed my life," said Rod Coffman, the 1955 state tournament starting guard. "I was kind of a screwed up kid — and continued to be screwed up for a couple of years actually — but the attention I received from Coach Saudargas made me feel that good things were going to happen. As it turned out, they did."

Rod Coffman, 51, leaps for a rebound while playmaker Rex Parker, 43, sets up in the backcourt. Coffman and Parker, teammates since grade school, combined to give the Warriors strong defense, devastating fast breaks, and potent outside shooting.

Go West, Young Man . . .

Fighting hard against the Warrior sophomores during the '52-'53 season was Rod Coffman, starting guard and high scorer on the East High team that tied with West for second place in Big Eight conference regular season play and vied with West for the top spot in the '53 Belvidere frosh-soph tournament. Coffman was slated to move up with his sophomore teammates to play varsity basketball at East, but he instead moved back across the river and ended up playing for East's archrival West High Warriors.

"It was late in my sophomore year when we moved back to the West Side," Coffman said. "My intent was to continue going to East High because school district rules permitted students to continue at their original high school if their families moved. The problem for me was the long, twice-daily commute. It took me forever to get to East. I lived close to West High and had to catch a bus downtown, then transfer to another bus. At the end of the day, I had to do the same thing in reverse. If I played sports or did anything after school, I didn't get home until 7:30 or 8 p.m. It was exhausting, and I was tired of it, but I started my junior year at East anyway and went out for the cross country team.

"After about three or four weeks of getting up very early in the morning and getting home very late at night, I decided that enough was enough. I was under a lot of pressure at East because the coaches were all trying to make sure I stayed there, including head basketball coach Jim Laude. Coach Laude called me into his office on two or three occasions and tried to talk me into staying, but it was just too difficult. Not only did I quit East, I also quit school.

"I got a factory job at Amerock where Marv Johnson took me under his wing. He was an East High graduate and a basketball star at Wheaton College, a CCI (College Conference of Illinois) All-Conference forward for four years and was named to the Helms College Basketball All-American team his senior year. I think he felt he could talk me into going back to East. I was sixteen years old, working at Amerock, playing basketball in the Industrial League with Marv, and learning a lot. Our team even went to Wheaton College and played their freshman team a couple times.

"Although I was well treated at Amerock, I was intending to go back to school the following semester the whole time I was there. Marv wanted me to go to East, but I decided to go to West because I lived only four blocks from the school and it was so much easier for me than commuting across town.

"I didn't know what to expect at West even though I knew a lot of people there. Rex Parker had been my childhood friend from the second grade on, and I had met other West High athletes through school and summer sports over the years. Bobby Washington and I were both selected for regional baseball honors and had traveled together to Chicago.

"Still, I was an outsider. I was not one of the guys coming back from the previous year's team and, of course, I couldn't play for West my junior year. Big Eight Conference rules required that players who transfer from another school must sit out a year.

"In the fall, some of us would play basketball on West's outdoor courts after classes while the football teams were on the practice fields behind the school. Coach Saudargas was sophomore football coach, and he would stop by to watch us play for 10 or 15 minutes when football practice ended.

"During the semester, I found out he was keeping tabs on me the same way he kept tabs on his players. Teachers would tell me, 'You know, Coach Saudargas was in here asking how you're doing and if you needed any help in anything.' When he saw me in the hallway, he would always ask, 'Coffman, how's everything? Are you doing okay? Do you feel comfortable here?' I'd always say, 'Yeah.' He'd never ask me about basketball. He just wanted to know how I was doing.

"I didn't say anything to him, but those were tough times for me. My parents were divorced. My father was a traveling salesman for the Hood Rubber Company and was gone most of the week. I was on my own, a kid 16 years old taking care of myself and my two younger brothers. That's too much responsibility and too much freedom for someone that age. A youngster in that situation doesn't always do the right thing. It helped me to know that Coach Saudargas was interested in me. He didn't have to do a lot, just those little comments, those little things, and it encouraged me.

"I thought maybe the fact that my whole junior year was wiped out when I transferred from East to West meant my basketball days were over, but Coach Saudargas made it clear in his way that I was still important and that maybe next year I could be part of the team. Because of that, I began to pull myself together. I'm very grateful to him for what he did for me.

"At one point, he went with me to James Blue, the principal, and made sure that I understood exactly what my eligibility rights were. He explained what the district and conference rule books said and made Mr. Blue sign off on it so everyone understood I would be eligible the following year. That in itself was encouragement, too. I felt if Coach Saudargas did that, he must be thinking that maybe I could play, but I knew that winning a starting position in my '54-'55 senior year was going to be difficult at the very least. The guys coming back who played for West the year before kind of knew who the starters were going to be, and I was interfering with that."

Coach Saudargas' son Alex said he remembers his father talking about Coffman, about his situation and about how quiet and reserved Coffman was when he first arrived at West. "Dad told me Coffman had gone to East and that it was hard to transfer to another school when you're a 16 or 17 year old. Your friends are at your old school and you don't feel comfortable at your new school, so you're a little shy. Dad encouraged Parker and Gentry and Grabow to stay on top of Coffman and to make sure he was feeling good about being at West. I saw Coffman's personality change a little from the time he first came to West. By the time they won the championship, he was becoming more outgoing."

Coffman said, "Over the next summer we played a lot of basketball on the outdoor court at Roosevelt Junior High with Wessels and Gentry and Grabow, and Parker and other very good players. Even some former Warrior stars like Bob Griggas, who had graduated and were playing college ball, came back and played. That summer I got to know and become friends with all the players at West, especially with John Wessels who practically lived at our house with me and my brothers.

"It seemed like every night Coach Saudargas would drive up and sit near the basketball court to watch. IHSA rules prohibited summer practices and coaching, so he wasn't able to coach us while we played. But we learned a lot during those games anyway because we had such a good mix of talented high school and college players.

"When basketball season finally came around, I knew there was a lot of pressure on Coach Saudargas because West had a set team coming back from the '53-'54 season and the returning players expected to be starters. Their fans expected them to be the starting lineup, too, and they weren't receptive to an outsider coming in, especially an outsider from the East Side. I think that's why I wasn't starting games at the beginning of the season. Of course, I was upset that I wasn't starting, but, in retrospect, I think Coach Saudargas did absolutely the right thing. By the time he worked me into the lineup and I became a starter, no one resented it."

The starting five . . .

When a reporter asked Coach Saudargas for a one line description of his 1955 state tournament starting five, he responded, "Rex Parker has that exceptional something. Rod Coffman is our great gift from our friends on the east side of the river. Fred Boshela has come through like he owns the place. John Wessels has one of the finest basketball shooting touches God ever gave a boy. And Nolden Gentry is one of the finest basketball players and finest men ever born."

Left: High-scoring Johnny Wessels, 44, shows off the hook shot that prompted sportswriters to dub him "Magic Touch." Right: High-flying Nolden Gentry, 45, launches a jump shot over a defender.

High Hopes, Higher Expectations

Rockford's West High Warriors were the talk of the town -- and of the entire state -- when the '54-'55 high school basketball season opened, with press associations rating them the number one team in Illinois. Their reputation even spread to other states when Abe Saperstein, owner-coach of the Harlem Globetrotters, was quoted in a national sports weekly referring to West High and citing Illinois basketball as the best in the country. "I'm the most traveled guy in the business and probably see more basketball than anyone else," Saperstein said. "But it's always the kid from Illinois the college coaches want to know about. It seems as if the boys from Illinois go on to be great in college, too. For example, no matter where I go, the coaches keep asking me about Nolden Gentry of West Rockford High School."

So packed with talent were the towering Warriors that one Chicago sportswriter said the greatest challenge Coach Saudargas faced was finding a way to "establish harmony on a roster loaded with individual stars, blending them into a unit that put the team ahead of other considerations." Coach Saudargas was well aware of the challenge.

Senior Warriors the preceding year had demonstrated that not everyone is willing to put team first and self second. When Coach Saudargas brought junior varsity guard Rex Parker up to the varsity in midseason and inserted him into the starting lineup, two top senior reserves objected to being "passed over" and quit the team. They told their coach they did not think they were being treated fairly because they were in their last year at West while Parker, a junior, would have another season to play. Senior starting guard Ray Paul, who was benched to make room for Parker, chose to stay with the team, though Paul was not accustomed to sitting on the bench in any sport. He lettered in football, basketball, and baseball all three years at West and was known as an intense, spirited athlete whose head and heart were always in the game.

Parker described Paul as "the epitome of the three sport man who was idolized by all the younger players at Roosevelt and West. When Coach Saudargas was teaching us how to rebound, how to get in position and block out our opponent, he would say, 'Watch Ray Paul' as the model to follow."

Paul later recalled how Saudargas went about benching him. "I think what happened is a reflection on Coach Saudargas and the insight he had into individuals and players," Paul said. "When I was a junior in the '52-'53 season, I played forward because I was the second tallest guy on the team at 6'1". The next year we had Wally Miller at 6'5", Gentry at 6'6", Boshela at 6'4", and Grabow at 6'4", so Coach Saudargas put me at guard for a good portion of the year. Nobody jelled, and we were just a so-so team.

"I had a little bit of a temper and a mouth that was worse than the temper. After we had lost to East High for the second time that year, I was full of myself because I had scored 15 points. That was a lot of points for me, and I was pretty excited about it. Right after the game, Coach Saudargas took me aside and said, 'You shot too much.' That immediately set me off. When we started arguing and I said, 'The only reason I play basketball is because it's something to do between football and baseball,' Coach Saudargas said, 'Paul, you're benched.' That was it. Rex played the whole time the rest of the year and I didn't play again until the regional tournament.

"Later I figured out — and Coach Saudargas admitted — that I had fallen into his trap. Rex was a much better player to begin with, but it was a problem to play Rex ahead of me because I was a senior. In the end, Rex got the experience he needed to prepare for the championship season. I thought it was a clever thing for Coach Saudargas to do. He understood kids and he understood what he wanted to do as a coach, and he could spot where he needed stronger players. He knew how to teach them what they needed to do, and he had the ability to motivate players to do it. Playing for him was one of those great learning experiences you carry with you all your life."

West's clever coach was matched the next year with an extraordinary assembly of gifted athletes. Among players taking the court for West High at the start of the '54-'55 season along with senior Rex Parker at guard were some big guns well known to fans from past exploits. Other returning lettermen included senior guard Don Grabow, senior forward Fred Boshela, who was third-highest scorer in the Big Eight Conference the preceding year, and junior forward Nolden Gentry, who had come to West after always being a leading scorer in junior high. Joining them was junior center John Wessels, who was high scorer for West's sophomore team the year before. Crosstown transfer Coffman brought his own high scorer exploits to the Warriors from his junior high and East High years.

As if handling all that talent wasn't challenge enough, Coach Saudargas had to explain himself to anxious fans and parents. He told a reporter, "I have parents calling up and wanting to know why their boy didn't get to play more or get to shoot more or why someone else was shooting more than others and so on."

"He would have tons of parents and onlookers up there watching at every basketball practice," Alice said, "and they were always calling up or coming down to give him advice: 'You know, you need to do this or you need to do that or why are you playing this person, why are you doing this?' He was always very polite to them and would say, 'I appreciate what you said. I'll take it under advisement and think about it. Thank you.'"

When the year started, Coffman was on the bench while Parker and Grabow were the starting guards. Coach Saudargas worked Coffman into the lineup bit by bit, then moved him into the starting guard position when Grabow was sidelined for several weeks with a kidney infection. When

Grabow returned, he didn't get back into the starting lineup. Instead he accepted a new role assigned to him by Coach Saudargas. Grabow, who excelled as sixth man, described in his journal how Coach Saudargas handled the situation.

"I did my part to help the team at the beginning of the season, but then I began to feel very tired all the time and I began to lose weight. I was so intent on keeping my starting position that I just kept on trying harder without telling anyone of my pain and the problems my body was giving me. Doctors my dad took me to said I had the flu. When things didn't get better, my dad finally took me to the Monroe Clinic in Monroe, WI. They found a virus had settled in my kidneys and told me I had to stay in bed for at least six weeks.

"Slowly my strength returned so I could go back to school and basketball. Coach Saudargas explained that my ability to handle the ball, to rebound, and to make perfectly placed passes meant that I was of greater value to the team playing in all the positions instead of just playing guard." Grabow often came off the bench throughout the remainder of the regular season and in championship games to make major contributions.

From that time on, Coach Saudargas had his starting five in place with no dissension and with the entire team working smoothly.

Trial by fire . . .

Coach Saudargas and his Warriors had no time for basking in the glory of preseason media hype. Eager to challenge Warrior hopes with the opening tipoff of the new season were the highly touted Moline Maroons, fresh from a disappointing 73-59 loss in the '54 state tournament finals to the reigning state champion Mt. Vernon Rams. Illinois sportswriters favored Moline to make a return visit to the '55 finals in March and considered the matchup a possible preview of the 1955 state championship title game. Rockford sportswriter Jim Johnston described the West High-Moline encounter as "the most attractive opener Illinois prep basketball has seen in years."

West High's Warriors were loaded with talent, and Coach Saudargas experimented with player combinations before settling on this starting five for regular season and tournament play. Left to right are guard, 43, Rex Parker; center, 44, Johnny Wessels; forward, 45, Nolden Gentry; forward, 53, Fred Boshela; and guard, 51, Rod Coffman.

Success Brings New Challenges

Thousands of prep athletes at more than 900 Illinois high schools took to the hardwood in the late fall of 1954 with the same dream: to win the coveted, single class state basketball championship at Champaign-Urbana the following spring. No season opener generated more tournament talk than the invasion of West High's home-court by the perennial basketball powerhouse from Moline. The nonconference game pitted against each other two talented teams mentored by two future Illinois coaching Hall-of-Famers, West's Saudargas and the Moline Maroon's Jack Foley.

Warrior fans had some anxious moments after the tipoff as West floundered with first game mistakes and jitters. Moline jumped off to an early lead and dominated the opening minutes of play, but Warrior sharpshooters came to life midway through the first quarter and tied the game at 12. After Warrior guard Rex Parker gave West its first lead with a 25 footer from the corner in the closing minutes of the quarter, both teams turned their intensity up a notch and committed a flurry of fouls. Moline hit on five free throws and the Warriors on four in the last two minutes.

The quarter ended with West guard Don Grabow sinking a 30 foot shot that put the Warriors ahead to stay, 20-17.

The second quarter was all Warriors. To the delight of the high-spirited, full-house, hometown crowd, the Warriors took control of the boards while West's ballhawk guards Parker and Grabow joined forces to all but shut down Moline's offense. The Maroon's leading scorer, Whitey Verstraete, was held to only six points in the first two quarters while the Warriors surged ahead 34 to 25, searing the Nets with a .636 first half shooting percentage.

Verstraete returned to form in the second half after Parker and Grabow fouled out. They were replaced by junior guard Bobby Washington and Warrior newcomer Rod Coffman, but Verstraete's 26 point second half resurgence was too little too late. He and his Maroons could not keep pace with Warrior scoring. By the end of the third quarter, West had opened up a commanding 59-45 lead.

Midway through the fourth quarter West led by 19 points, 71 to 52, and Saudargas began emptying his bench, using all 15 players. Moline cut 11 points off West's lead in the final four minutes, but the Warrior's 74 to 66 victory was never in doubt.

Game summaries highlighted what was to become a familiar story for Warrior followers: Wessels was the high scorer with 26 points; Gentry and Boshela controlled the boards and played great defense; playmaker Parker, described by teammate Bobby Washington as a "street fighter" on defense, effectively stymied the Maroons' offense, fouling out in the process; Grabow deftly threaded the Maroon defense with spot on passes to the high scorers inside; junior Bobby Washington provided strong backup support at guard; and Rod Coffman played well on defense while chipping in points from the backcourt and corners whenever the defense fell back to shut down Warrior high scorers under the basket.

Saudargas and his Warriors entered the locker room after the game with the confidence that comes from knowing they had bested a good team. When they emerged from the locker room, Coach Saudargas and his Warriors encountered a new challenge. So glowing was the post-game praise heaped on the Warriors by coach Foley that it would make West an upset target of every team they encountered for the rest of the season. "I don't see how they can lose a game this year," Foley told a Chicago sportswriter. "They are big, and I mean big. They can all move around and rebound well. If I had to pick a state champion now, I would say it would be Rockford West. This Nolden Gentry and John Wessels are really tough." It was high praise from the coach of the team that went on to win 17 in a row before being topped by Princeton at the state tournament.

Foley's prophecy gained credence in the four nonconference games that followed. West routed Chicago's Van Steuben 85 to 47 a week later despite losing their number one relief man in the forward wall, 6'5" senior Dave McClelland, who was sidelined with a concussion during a rough-and-tumble practice scrimmage. Van Steuben was never in the game as the Warriors showcased their balanced offense. Wessels again led Warriors' scoring with 19 points. Gentry added 17 and Boshela 14. Fans were treated to an encore performance the next night as the Warriors easily bested Belvidere 87 to 48. Wessels and Boshela shared scoring honors with 20 points each and guard Coffman came in right behind them at 17. Coach Saudargas used all 15 players both nights.

Only two nonconference games remained before Big Eight Conference opponents began putting the Warriors to sterner tests. First was a road game against the Rochelle Hubs, unbeaten in three games, but easily topped by the Warriors 75-51. Boshela lead the scoring with 21 points. Wessels chipped in 18 and Coffman 14.

In the final nonconference game of the preseason, West hosted one of Indiana's best teams, Gary's Lew Wallace Hornets, the first team able to challenge the Warriors' towering forward wall of 6'6" Gentry, 6'6" Wessels, and 6'4" Boshela. Starting at center for the Hornets was 6'9" Don Van Meter, aided under the boards by two 6'5' forwards, Don Wyatt and Keith Baron. It was literally a hard-fought game with elbowing and jostling under the boards, but the Warriors won the battle. The Hornets were unable to match Gentry in pulling down rebounds, which gave the Warriors the edge because both teams' shooting percentages were so low. West hit on only 23 of 68 shots, a .338 shooting percentage, a sharp fall from their .500 average during the first four games. Lew Wallace hit on only 17 of 65 shots for a .217 percentage. The pitched battle ended with West on top 68-49. Better rebounding and balanced scoring were the Warriors' keys to victory: Boshela and Wessels contributed 12 points each, Gentry and Grabow 11, and Coffman added eight.

Lew Wallace was just what Coach Saudargas and his Warriors needed to prepare for their Big Eight Conference opener the following week at Elgin, also undefeated in their nonconference tune-ups. Elgin's Maroons were always toughest when they had the home court advantage — and they were ready with a hostile greeting the moment the Warriors entered the gym.

The rise of "The Comeback Kids"

"My husband always told his players, 'You have to keep your eye on the prize and you have to work towards your goal and you just keep going and going and going and going. You are sure to meet adversity along the way, things are not always going to be wonderful, but you have to keep going and keep going and keep going. You have to work your way through it, and if you can't go through it, you have to figure out how to go around the thing to keep winning. If you persevere, and if you are committed and dedicated, you will get there and you will win.'"

— Alice Saudargas

"Welcome to the Lion's Den."

Coach Saudargas and his Warriors had to clear a long-standing hurdle in their opening Big Eight Conference game against the Elgin Maroons. Both teams had met and topped tough challengers to remain undefeated in their nonconference games, and both teams were highly rated by Illinois sportswriters. But both teams also knew that neither the Maroons nor the Warriors had ever lost to the other team at home, never in the history of the schools, and the Warriors were opening conference play on the Maroons' home court. Elgin players were ready and waiting with a hostile welcome for the Warrior invaders.

"At that time the Big Eight Conference was the toughest conference in the state, and we did a lot of traveling because the teams were 60, 70, 80 miles away from us," Warrior guard Rod Coffman said. "Our bus left West High mid-afternoon, so we arrived about 5:30. When we walked into the Elgin High School gym, nobody was there yet except the Elgin High School varsity team. They were sitting in the stands and throwing wise comments at us as we walked to the locker room. We couldn't believe it. There had to be 15 to 20 guys in there making insulting remarks at us. None of us said anything. We just walked into the locker room and got ready for the game. And that was it. We felt we were playing for the Big Eight championship when we played Elgin, and we had to win that game. We were only scheduled to play them once that year. Other teams we had to play twice, home and away, but we had only one game with Elgin that year, and it was at their gym."

Elgin's taunts seemed to have the desired effect. The Maroons jumped off to an early lead and forced the Warriors to play catch-up for the entire first quarter. The quarter ended with the score tied at 11, but it took two free throws by Warrior guard Rex Parker after the buzzer to pull the Warriors even with the Maroons.

Elgin's relentless onslaught continued. The Warriors were able to tie the score twice in the second quarter, but never took the lead. As the Warriors struggled against a very tight Maroon defense, Parker kept them in the game with eight straight free throws. The first half ended with Elgin on top 25-24, the first time the Warriors had found themselves behind in a game beyond first quarter action.

Matters grew worse in the third quarter, with Elgin outscoring West 18-14. It looked as though Warrior hopes for a conference championship and dreams of going downstate at tournament time were dying at the hands of a powerful Elgin team and the Elgin-Rockford visiting team's home court jinx. When the Warriors gathered around Coach Saudargas at the end of the third quarter, they found themselves down by five, 43-38.

It was the same Warrior players but a suddenly different Warrior team that took the court for the fourth quarter. Within the first two minutes, the Warriors came alive and surged ahead. Now it was Elgin's turn to play catch-up. With six minutes left to go, Elgin tied the score for the last time when their stalwart guard and playmaker Gary "Whitey" Smith sank two free throws. Seconds later the Warrior's Parker responded with a drive-in basket that put the Warriors ahead to stay. The Warriors were ahead by six at the final buzzer, 62-56.

Coach Saudargas used only his five starters and sixth man Grabow against Elgin, with every player pitching in for what sportswriters described as a full team performance that again showcased the balanced offense. Wessels was high scorer at 18 points, followed by Parker with 17. Boshela added 11, including chips-down, critical baskets in the fourth quarter. Gentry controlled the boards, especially in the fourth quarter, and contributed eight points. Coffman and Grabow were strong on defense and added six and two points respectively.

Elgin's tight defense held the Warriors to 56 shots from the floor and 19 baskets while the Maroons got off 71 shots for 21 baskets. Though the Warriors were outscored from the floor, they won the game from the free throw line, outscoring Elgin 24-14, with Parker (9) and Boshela (5) accounting for 14 between them.

Elgin had tested the Warrior's resolve and character as no one had before, and the Warriors passed with honors. Their 24 point blitzkrieg in the fourth quarter proved to be a prelude for things to come. They fell short of the torrid 78 point average they had before encountering Elgin, but their tenacity earned the Warriors a new nickname, "The comeback kids."

Warriors Forever

"Things didn't always go our way..."

"I joined the faculty at West High after returning from the service during the Korean War, and I attended every game, home and away. Things didn't always go our way, but what separated the Warriors from others was a thing called character. They were a disparate group with diverse backgrounds and family situations coming together under a coach who was also a great mentor. Every person on that squad and every person connected with the team derived some personal benefit from knowing Coach Saudargas, benefits that paid immediate dividends on the court and lifelong dividends beyond."

— Keith Irons, West High Faculty

Warriors Forever

Whatever It Takes

Elgin was a tough hurdle to clear, but the Warriors' schedule, described by sportswriter Jim Johnston as "one of the most rigorous 20-game schedules ever encountered by a Rockford basketball team before tournament time," included six more Big Eight Conference teams and five nonconference foes that could be just as tough or tougher than Elgin. Big Eight opponents watching and probing for any Warrior weaknesses were the LaSalle-Peru Cavaliers, Joliet Steelmen, Aurora East Tomcats, Aurora West Blackhawks, Freeport Pretzels, and the E-Rabs of Rockford East, the Warriors' hometown archrival across the Rock River. Two of the Warriors' Big Eight opponents had experience in recent state tournament action. Freeport won the 1951 state championship and had a shot at defending their title the next year, but were defeated by Quincy in the finals. Quincy lost the championship game that year to the smallest school ever to win the state trophy, the Hebron Green Giants. Rockford's E-Rabs were the reigning Big Eight Conference champions and made it to the 1954 state championship finals in Champaign-Urbana before being eliminated in the quarterfinals by Moline.

Even the Elgin Maroons were not done with the Warriors yet; an unscheduled opportunity to avenge their home court loss lay ahead, a history making, no-holds-barred, take-no-prisoners battle for the 1955 state championship three months down the road with the eyes of the entire state on them. "Our league was so tough," West's sophomore basketball coach Don Krieschbaum said, "that when we got downstate or in the bigger sectional tournaments, we were ready; 1955 was a good example. How often do two teams from the same conference defeat all challengers from every other part of the state and end up slugging it out in the championship game?"

Probing for Warrior weaknesses — and finding one — were the LaSalle-Peru Cavaliers, the Warriors' next Big Eight challengers. The Cavaliers traveled to Rockford for a midweek battle, the last game before school was dismissed for the holidays. West High's gym was packed with excited and expectant fans welcoming their Warriors home and celebrating the end of the Elgin home court jinx. Their Warriors were now holding not only the top spot in the Big Eight Conference, but also the top spot on the Associated Press ranking of all high school basketball teams in the state of Illinois. Warrior mania did not intimidate the upset-minded Cavaliers though, and they quickly put a damper on Warrior enthusiasm.

The game was even at the start, and the Warriors gradually started edging ahead to a five

Rex Parker drives in with a layup to stave off the Cavaliers' attack.

point lead at the end of the first quarter. But that was when the Cavaliers opened fire over the heads of the taller Warrior forward wall. They attacked with long range shots that brought them even with the Warriors, and the lead changed hands 10 times in the second quarter. The Cavaliers had a 30-29 lead late in the period, but a bucket by center Johnny Wessels, two free throws by forward Nolden Gentry and a swisher by guard Rod Coffman as time ran out gave the Warriors a 35-30 halftime edge.

Cavalier sharpshooters were not able to sustain their long range accuracy in the second half and the Warriors took charge, showcasing their balanced offense once again. "Magic Touch" Wessels, as sportswriters started calling him, dropped in 25 points. Gentry hit on 11 of 12 free throws and chipped in three from the floor to end with 17 points. Coffman added 14, Fred Boshela 10, and Rex Parker seven. Once again Coach Saudargas used all 15 players as the Warriors posted a sizzling .600 shooting percentage from the floor and coasted to a 79-63 win.

After the LaSalle-Peru game, no conference action was slated for 16 days while school was out. During the break, the Warriors hosted two Indiana teams in Rockford for the annual East High-West High round robin Christmas tournament. But the next test of Warrior character did not come from the Hoosier State, it fell from the sky; it came not on the basketball court, but on snowbound streets as Rockford was buried under eight inches of snow on game day, halting traffic and forcing motorists to abandon cars in snowdrifts.

"We played Hammond Tech the first night of the tournament," Warrior forward Nolden Gentry said. "It snowed all afternoon and evening before the game. I had my father's 1939 Plymouth, and I picked up a couple teammates, Bobby Washington and Don Slaughter, and we headed for the game. Traffic was backed up and cars were having trouble getting up hills. There must have been five or six inches of snow on the ground by then.

"After traveling about an hour and a half for what usually was a 10 minute trip, and not even being halfway there yet, we decided to take some side streets to get away from the snarled traffic. We ended up getting stuck, and by that time were late for the game even though the storm delayed starting time about 90 minutes.

"There was no way that I was going to miss the game. We were undefeated and had defeated Moline and Elgin, the two top teams in Northern Illinois, and were dreaming of an undefeated season. In 1953-54, I came down with tonsillitis during the week leading up to the East-West game. The doctors held me out of the game, and we lost. I did not want that to happen again."

Warrior guard Rod Coffman echoed the same resolve: "There was never a thought of not being there," he said. "The game was everything. I would have gotten out of the car and started running if I had to. That's how important it was. I probably would have been exhausted after running through the deep snow, but I would have gotten there because it was so important, especially a game against an Indiana team. We had heard so much about Indiana basketball and how strong they were. I wanted to make sure I got there.

"We had been in the house all day and saw that it was snowing, but we didn't realize how bad the storm was. My father and I usually picked up Wessels, so I called John to let him know it was time to leave and we were on the way. He lived only a couple miles from us, but we realized when we were about halfway there that we couldn't make it. The snowdrifts were too high and cars were stuck or abandoned everywhere. We tried several ways to get through, but we were getting stuck every few minutes and had to push our way out. Finally we were near a store — we didn't have cell phones then — so I went in and called John. I told him to start walking toward the gym and we would pick him up. We never found him. I had to walk the last five or six blocks to the gym because all the cars had stopped. They couldn't make it uphill, and neither could my father's car. He didn't have snow tires or chains, and just couldn't get through the snow. John came into the gym a few minutes after I arrived. He was a little upset, but somebody had picked him up."

In the meantime, Gentry said he and his teammates "got my father's car pushed to the curb and started walking through snow that in some areas was up to our knees. When we got to the gym, the game had started, but was still in the first quarter."

Coffman said, "Some players didn't arrive till about halftime, but everyone fought to get there. Hammond Tech had come into Rockford before the storm and checked in to a hotel downtown. It took their bus more than two hours through the snow-clogged streets to get from the hotel to the gym two miles away, normally a six minute drive, but they were already there. So were the fans. It was amazing. The gym was completely jam-packed. Somehow they found a way to get there. It may not have been totally full at the beginning of the game, but by the end of the first quarter it was packed. That's how intense the interest was."

Even though most of the Warriors had trudged through heavy snow at least part of the way to the game, they were unfazed and indomitable. They seemed strengthened by adversity. With overpowering, in-your-face defense, the Warriors held the Hoosier visitors to only one point in the first quarter and seven in the second. By the end of the third quarter, the Warriors held a commanding 42-22 lead, then outscored Hammond 23-9 in the fourth to wrap up a 65-31 rout.

It was a physical battle, with the Warriors committing 17 fouls — four by Grabow and Wessels, three by Parker, and two by Gentry and Washington. Hammond committed 13 fouls. High scorer for the Warriors, despite spending the first quarter slogging through snowdrifts and playing less than three quarters in the game, was Nolden Gentry with 17 points. Wessels contributed 15, Boshela 5, and Grabow 8.

It was not a blinding snowstorm that greeted the Hoosier visitors from Gary Froebel on the second night of the Christmas tournament. It was a blinding Warrior offense. The Warriors raced to a 61-35 halftime lead that grew to 88-50 by the end of the third quarter. By evening's end, the Warriors had scored a 99-74 victory and had set three records while dazzling their Hoosier visitors with a display of Illinois basketball at its best:

1. It was the highest score (99) ever posted by a single team on West High's home court;

2. It was the highest combined score (173) ever posted at West;

3. It was the highest score (99) ever posted by a Warrior team during the regular season.

Fans chanted for the Warriors to break the 100 point mark, but Coach Saudargas chose to keep his five starters and sixth man on the bench the entire fourth quarter. Even playing only three quarters, Wessels had led the scoring with 31 points. Boshela chipped in 18, Gentry 16, and Parker 11.

The Warriors sent their Hoosier guests packing back to Indiana with some unforgettable Illinois memories, and Warrior confidence was heightened when polls by both the Associated Press and United Press International named the Warriors the number one team in the state. But that good news was followed by bad news the following week as the Warriors returned to Big Eight Conference play at East Aurora, then prepared for a home court battle with their nemesis from Rock Island. It was the Rock Island Rocks who had derailed the 7-0 Warriors a year earlier and started them on a downhill slide that included five losses in their next 12 games.

"Just a bunch of kids until . . ."

"I just hope that if the Warriors do get scalped, the scalping is done before tournament time so they'll have a chance to bounce back. They truly are of state championship caliber, but like anybody else, just a bunch of kids until they prove themselves at Champaign."
— Rockford Register-Republic Sports Editor Jim Johnston

Warriors Forever

Negative Results Are Positive Too.

Coach Saudargas and his high-flying Warriors faced still another challenge when they returned to action in January against East Aurora. Don Grabow, the Warriors' stalwart, 6'4" sixth man who filled in flawlessly whenever and wherever needed was sidelined for at least a month with a kidney infection. With Grabow out and the state tournament only eight weeks away, Saudargas decided to take a longer look at three senior reserves — 6'2" forward Tom Olson, 6'5" center Dave McClelland, and 5'11 guard Ray Morgan. — who were battling five juniors for positions on the 10-player tourney squad. Another candidate to fill Grabow's spot was 5'10"senior guard Luther Bedford, who missed pre-holiday action after suffering a football leg injury in the fall but was ready to suit up for the East Aurora game.

East Aurora's Tomcats had lost their first five games and were at the bottom of the Big Eight Conference. Coach Saudargas warned his players that the Tomcats were better than their record indicated and that they were always tough on their home court. They had won their last two games and had held a 34 to 29 halftime lead over the powerful Elgin five before the Maroons rallied to victory in the second half.

Tomcats' coach Ewald Metzger buoyed up his players — and also may have inadvertently fired up the Warriors — with his prediction that no Big Eight team was good enough to finish the season undefeated in conference play. As the game started, it looked as though coach Metzger's Tomcats were going to back up his prediction. The Tomcats scored six straight points, and held an 11 to 6 lead midway through the first quarter.

That's when the Warriors erupted with a record surge, unleashing a devastating wallop with a 22 point scoring rampage, making the score 28 to 11 before the Tomcats scored again. Gentry started it with two free throws and poured in seven points during the barrage. Wessels added six, Boshela five, Coffman three, and Parker topped off the drive with a free throw.

Free throws became a big part of the game at that point when foul after foul turned the contest into a melee with a total of 48 fouls, 19 by the Warriors and 29 by the Tomcats, including two East Aurora technical fouls. The Warriors scored 31 points from the free throw line and the Tomcats 13. The scuffle ended with the Warriors on top 81-47.

Four Tomcat starters fouled out of the game. The only Warrior to foul out was ace defender and in-your-face ballhawk Rex Parker. His aggressive play had landed him on the bench once before in the hard fought season opener against Moline, and he was the only Warrior starter to foul out during the Warriors' 10 game winning streak.

Gentry led Warrior scoring with 27 points, followed by Wessels with 22 and Boshela 15. Coffman added 9 and Parker 6. Coach Saudargas used his entire 15-player squad in the game.

While the Warriors emerged on top in their skirmish with the Tomcats, Elgin's Maroons handed East Rockford's E-Rabs their first loss of the season, leaving the undefeated Warriors alone at the top of the Big Eight Conference. Elgin, East Rockford, Joliet, and LaSalle-Peru were in a four way tie for second place.

Jubilant and expectant Warrior fans filled the West High gym the following night to greet their triumphant Warriors, undefeated through 10 games, holding first place alone in the Big Eight Conference, and rated the number one team in the state by both the Associated Press and United Press International.

Visiting Rockford for the first Warrior home game of the new year and kicking off the second half of the 20-game pre-tournament season were the Rock Island Rocks, a nonconference foe struggling through the season with six wins and four losses. As Coach Saudargas had done before the battle with East Aurora, he warned his players that won-lost records mean nothing, that every opponent is a test and a threat demanding your best effort, and that any team can beat any other team on any given day or night — as Rock Island had demonstrated on their own home court the year before when they upset the highly favored Warriors 42-41.

The Rocks wasted no time validating Coach Saudargas' warning and took up where they left off the last time the two teams met. Rock Island outpositioned, outrebounded, outshot, and outhustled the flat-footed Warriors from the opening tipoff, scoring 10 straight and closing out the quarter ahead 22-9. They ran up an18 point lead, 31-13, midway through the second quarter before West responded with a full court press that cut the lead to 14 points, 41-27 at the half.

West outscored the Rocks 18 to 11 in the third quarter, then pulled within three points, 60-57, with three and half minutes to go in the game. Just when it looked as though the Warriors were on their way to another storybook finish, Gentry was called for charging. The Rocks sank two free throws, then scored twice from the field to take a 66-57 lead with 2:15 to go. The Warriors managed to outscore the Rocks 9 to 6 as the clock wound down, but time ran out on them and the final tally was 72-66.

Postgame analyses noted that West lost the game on the free throw line, hitting only 50 percent of their 20 free throw attempts. Making only six of the 10 missed free throws would have covered their six point losing margin. Meanwhile the Rocks hit on 83 percent of their free throws, 20 of 24. The Warriors outscored the Rocks from the field, hitting 28 of 68 while the Rocks hit on 26 of 50.

Coach Saudargas used only his five starters in the game from the opening tipoff to the final buzzer. Missing from the Warrior bench in addition to sixth man Grabow was junior reserve guard Bobby Washington who took to the court for the jayvee team before the varsity contest. While the Warriors had trouble scoring in the main event, Washington had a banner night with the jayvees, an indication of things to come, scoring 28 points on 12 baskets and four free throws in leading his team to a 50-47 victory over the Rock Island junior varsity. Washington was suited up with the varsity for the rest of the season.

Sportswriters covering the game cited two factors that led to the Warriors' defeat:

1. The Rocks' performance was so outstanding that they could have defeated many good teams that night.

2. The Warriors' first half performance was so poor that any good team could have run up a big lead over them. It cost them the game, though they fought through to the end.

Alice Saudargas described her husband's reaction to the loss. "The kids played kind of lackadaisically against Rock Island," she said. "They believed they were going to win as they always had, so they didn't really play as hard as they needed to. But Alex never blamed the kids. He just pointed out the things they had to do differently to win and cautioned them about being too cocky and too self-confident."

Looking to the future, Rockford newspaper columnist and sports editor Jim Johnston said, "The only question now seems to be just how they will react to their first setback. When a team riding as high as the Warriors were tastes defeat for the first time, one of two things usually happens," :

"1. The setback serves as a good lesson, and that team is tougher than ever.

"2. The team falls apart and loses several before regaining stride."

Coach Saudargas responded to Johnston with an optimistic note: "If they take it with the proper attitude, it will help. If not, it could hurt. I think our kids will take it right."

Even the pizza lost its flavor

"I remember after the Rock Island game we went to Maria's for pizza, but for the first time that season the pizza did not taste very good."
— *Rod Coffman, Warrior '55 starting guard*

Warriors Forever

Keeping Eyes on the Prize

After losing to Rock Island, the Warriors were no longer regarded as the undisputed number one team in the state. The Associated Press dropped the Warriors to third place. United Press International's poll kept them in the top spot, but not with the unanimous vote they had received before the loss. They were given only a slight margin over second-ranked Pinckneyville by UPI.

"I remember the loss to Rock Island like it was yesterday," said starting guard Rod Coffman. "We had gone into that game undefeated, the number one rated team in the state, and we were playing on our home court on a Saturday night. We ran into a team, an average team actually, that was struggling to play .500 basketball that year. But they were a hot shooting team that night and they had a couple guards who were hitting everything from beyond the circle. Every time we narrowed their lead, they would hit two or three long shots and we would fall further behind again. When we couldn't pull it out at the end, we began to realize for the first time that we were not invincible. We never took any game for granted from then on."

Rex Parker, Coffman's counterpart at guard, echoed that assessment. "We had things going pretty much our own way until then, and maybe we were a little overconfident. That game knocked us down a peg."

"You have to feel down after losing," sophomore coach Don Kriechbaum said, "but it's the comeback that's important. You take your kids and teach them to look beyond what happened, to work harder. You can erase a loss by winning your next one. It's part of coaching, and Alex was good at that."

The Warriors came roaring back with a vengeance in their next game, routing Freeport's Pretzels 85-56. The attack was led by Gentry with 19 points, scoring with six field goals and hitting on seven of 10 from the free throw line. Boshela chipped in 15, Wessels 14. Coffman 12, and new sixth man Bobby Washington 11. Their eagerness to erase the loss even showed up in Warrior fouling tallies: Parker fouled out after contributing seven points and thwarting Pretzel efforts on offense. Gentry fouled out for the first time in the season. Coffman was one short of fouling out, and three others, Boshela, Wessels, and reserve Dave McClelland fouled twice. All 15 Warriors got into the game. The win kept the Warriors in the top spot on the United Press International poll and moved the team from third place to second place in Associated Press ratings.

Next up was a home court contest with visiting archrival East Rockford, played before a rafter-shaking full house that sports editor Jim Johnston said, "left thousands of disappointed fans unable to get tickets for the crosstown classic." The E-Rabs were injury hobbled and struggling through the year with a 7-6 season record, 2-2 in conference play, under their new coach, Steve Polaski. East High's celebrated, perennial Coach Jim Laude, who had been at the helm since the school was opened in 1940, retired the previous year after winning the Big Eight Conference and taking his E-Rabs downstate but losing to Moline in the first round of the 1954 tournament. Two E-Rab reserves from that team were the only returning lettermen Polaski inherited, and he was having trouble putting together a consistent winning combination.

With the E-Rabs' ace rebounder and tallest player, 6'3" Fred Clow, out with a leg injury, the Warriors entered the contest with a four and a half inch height advantage per position. Despite the Warriors' height advantage, the E-Rabs bottled up Gentry, Wessels, and Boshela at the start. Unable to feed their tall, front line high scorers under the basket, Coffman and Parker launched a stunning, rapid fire, outside-shooting attack. Coffman hit twice from the back court, then Parker hit twice, then Coffman hit three in a row to put the Warriors ahead 24-4 at the end of the first quarter. That was when the E-Rab front line defense began to unravel. Gentry and Boshela started hitting, and the 20 point lead grew to 29 points, 38-11 at the half, then to 36 points, 55-19 at the end of the third quarter. When the final buzzer sounded, the Warriors were up by 44 points, 69 to 25. Coffman, the Warriors' East High transfer student, was the game's high scorer with 18 points. Boshela added 17 and Gentry 14, but East High's defense completely throttled Wessels, the Warriors' primary offensive weapon and leading scorer for the season, holding him to only two points — a success noted and imitated by future Warrior foes.

After the blowout victories over Freeport and East High, Coach Saudargas hatched a plan to thwart any return of the overconfidence that led to the Rock Island upset.

"Coach Saudargas never criticized us," Coffman said, "not even after losing to Rock Island. He didn't have to. He found a way to let someone else tell us what we needed to hear, someone with the power to get us fired up.

"On Monday, he gathered us in the hallway outside the gym and told us a story about a phone conversation he just had with his friend Dolph Stanley, who watched us play against East High. Anyone who grew up in Rockford was familiar with Dolph Stanley. He was one of basketball's living legends, and all of us were awed by him."

Rockford news reports often featured Stanley and his coaching exploits at Beloit College, just across the Wisconsin border, about 15 minutes north of Rockford. He coached Beloit College to six straight Midwest Collegiate Athletic Conference championships, won a berth in the 1951 National Invitation Tournament, and had a 238-57 record during 12 seasons there. Even before going to Beloit College, Stanley had won fame throughout Illinois by coaching three different high schools into postseason state tournaments and winning the 1944 state championship with Taylorville High School, the state's first undefeated state champion.

Taylorville's 45-0 season stands as an unchallenged state record because teams now play fewer games. Stanley later coached two more high schools to the state tournament, Auburn and Boylan Central Catholic, both in Rockford. He was inducted into the Illinois Basketball Coaches Association Hall of Fame as one of the winningest coaches in Illinois basketball history and was named All-Time Illinois High School Coach by the Chicago Tribune. Stanley also was inducted into the Wisconsin Basketball Coaches Association Hall of Fame for his successes at Beloit College.

Saudargas and Stanley had been friends for years. Bob Reitsch, one of the 1951-52 Warriors' leading scorers along with Bob Griggas, said Coach Saudargas had provided Stanley with several Warrior-groomed standouts for Beloit's championship teams and some of them came back to join in Warrior practices during breaks. Rex Parker cited Rockford West alums LaVerne Schuneman and All-State Warrior Clarence "Sour" Anderson among those who went on to play under Stanley and said, "Like other Rockford fans, we would go up to Beloit from time to time for Beloit Buccaneers' games.

"So," Coffman said, "when Coach Saudargas gathered us all together and told us that Dolph Stanley had told him some things about us he thought we should know, we paid attention."

"He said Stanley told him we had plenty of talent, but that he wasn't sure we had the drive or determination to be state champions. Coach Saudargas was a great psychologist and never wanted to bring negative things out, but he told the story so that he wasn't the one saying it, and the one who was saying it was someone who was well respected by all of us. He told us Stanley said we were a good team and that we could be the state champions, but we had to get ourselves up to another level.

"I don't know what impact that had on the other guys, but it had an impact on me. If somebody like Stanley, who was a really good coach, would say that about us, then there must be some truth to it. I just thought, 'Man, we have to work harder. I have to work harder from here on out.'

"We talked about it a few times, and I felt we got better, that we were stronger as a team after that. We became more focused and more intense at practice."

Parker said, "From then on we kept in mind that our ultimate goal was to win the state championship, but doing that meant every one of us had to play full-out every minute we were on the court."

Two basketball coaching Hall-of-Famers, Dolph Stanley, left, and Alex Saudargas, were living legends and lifelong friends. Several West High greats groomed by Coach Saudargas were sent north from Rockford after graduation to play for Stanley's nationally ranked teams at Beloit College, just 30 minutes from West High. Stanley cooperated with Coach Saudargas' strategy for lighting a fire under his Warrior championship teams. Later they entertained Rockford's basketball fans with media-hyped rivalries and raillery when Stanley took up residence in Rockford and coached Warrior rival schools Auburn and Boylan.

What makes a team?

"Johnny Wessels is one of the finest shooters you can find, able to hit from anywhere with a slight flip of the wrist. Nolden Gentry is as fine an all-around performer as I've seen. He has no peer as a rebounder, is tops defensively, and can score handily. Fred Boshela is an all-around standout, rugged under the boards, dangerous at the hoop. Rod Coffman is a fine outside shot and, with Rex Parker, provides a mighty fast, fast break. Parker is a real defensive stalwart in the back court. If that combination doesn't make a team, what does? The coach. Alex Saudargas is one of the finest in the state His record ranks with the best. Even the finest material needs careful development and screening, astute direction and guidance. Alex provides all that."
— *Rockford Register-Republic Sports Editor Jim Johnston*

*When Warrior foes tied up high-scoring center Johnny Wessels,
forward Fred Boshela, and forward Nolden Gentry near the basket,
guards Rex Parker, 43, and Rod Coffman, 51, started pouring in points
from beyond the free throw circle. When defenders came out to stop
them, Parker and Coffman again began feeding the ball to the high
scorers inside.*

The Stretch Run

With his Warriors strengthened for the final games of the regular season and firmly focused on the ultimate prize, Coach Saudargas began experimenting with ways to maximize Warrior potency.

He started by changing his center-jump lineup to give the Warriors more control of games at tipoffs and more scoring opportunities, a critical advantage in close games. Because forward Nolden Gentry was slightly taller and had a longer reach than center Johnny Wessels, Coach Saudargas moved Gentry into the center circle for jumps and moved Wessels to forward.

He also started experimenting with substitutions in preparation for trimming his 15-player squad to the 10-player limit allowed in postseason competition. His 5'9" sixth man Bobby Washington, who stepped in when Don Grabow was sidelined by illness, had been a capable replacement for Parker and Coffman at guard, but Coach Saudargas sought more height to back up his tall front line. His options, in addition to 6'5" Grabow when he returned to action, included 6'5" senior Dave McClelland, 6'2" senior Tom Olson, 6'2" junior Don Slaughter, 6'2" junior Joe DiGiovanni, 6'0" senior Sam Black, and 5'11" junior Sam Patton. Backups at guard, in addition to Washington, included 5'10" senior Luther Bedford and 5'10" senior Ray Morgan.

First to face the Warriors after Coach Saudargas gave them his Dolph Stanley-inspired pep talk was West Aurora. The Blackhawks were at the bottom of the Big Eight Conference with a 5-14 season record and no conference wins. Like several previous Warrior foes, the Blackhawks started the game with a zone defense and a ball-control offense, passing the ball around in the backcourt and not shooting until they had a good chance to connect, but it was futile. Parker and Coffman stole the ball six times in the first quarter and the Warriors capitalized to take a 15-6 lead at the buzzer.

With the Blackhawks' zone defense clogging up the middle and tying up Warrior high scorers on the front line, Coffman and Parker started shooting from the outside. Coffman poured in 15 points and Parker added ten. By halftime the Warriors led 29-13. When the Blackhawks adjusted their defense, Wessels broke open to pump in 22 points, Gentry nine, and Boshela seven. Blackhawk sharpshooters were hitting at an impressive . 528 rate, but they could not keep pace with the Warriors. The lead grew to 49-32 at the end of the third quarter, and the final tally was 64-52. All the Warrior reserves saw action in the fourth quarter.

Coach Saudargas discovered another weapon for his arsenal the following night as his Warriors warmed up for their nonconference contest with the 8-7 DeKalb Barbs. "Certain team rules my husband imposed on his players were non-negotiable," Alice Saudargas said. "An example was his no-smoking rule. Any player caught smoking was immediately kicked off the team because smoking undermined their conditioning and performance. Other rules were a sort of code of conduct and were not so rigidly enforced. They were open to change if he saw evidence a change could help the team."

One of Coach Saudargas' code of conduct rules discouraged horseplay such as dunking during warm-ups. Player interviews for a video produced by Rockford School District staffer Ron Johnson recalling the Warriors' 1955 season, describe a Coach Saudargas rule-changing incident that happened as the Warriors warmed up to play DeKalb. Coach Saudargas was standing with his back to the Warriors while he talked with the DeKalb coach. Suddenly the crowd roared when one of the Warriors went in for a slam dunk. Coach Saudargas turned around, but saw nothing. Then the same thing happened a second time and the crowd went wild. Finally Coach Saudargas caught Wessels going in for a dunk. While Coach Saudargas was standing there glaring at Wessels, Gentry went in and dunked with both hands. "Coach Saudargas was angry then and was standing there with his hands on his hips," a Warrior told Johnson. "When he put his hands on his hips, you knew you were in trouble. I was looking down the other way, and the DeKalb feed line was falling apart. Their players were standing around watching us while balls were hitting them in the chest and going into the stands. I said, 'Coach, this game is over. Look down there.' He looked and said, 'I believe you're right!' From then on, that was part of the routine, and I mean it was kind of terrifying if you were on the other side."

The Warriors took advantage of the awed Barbs and scored 10 straight points in the first quarter. The game was no contest as the Warriors led 18-7 at the end of the quarter, 35-19 at the half, and 48-27 after three quarters. The Barbs outscored the Warriors 16-15 in the final period as Coach Saudargas played all of his reserves, closing out the Warriors' 14th victory, 63-43. Wessels dumped in 21 points, Gentry 15, and Coffman 10.

With victories over West Aurora and DeKalb, the Warriors returned to the number one spot in the Associated Press poll. Perennial powerhouse Pinckneyville had taken over AP's number one rating after the Warriors lost to Rock Island, but fell to second place behind the Warriors over the weekend after suffering a 15 point drubbing by Centralia. United Press International's poll continued rating the Warriors number one, as they had done since the start of the season.

As if to mock those ratings, LaSalle-Peru's Cavaliers very nearly pulled off an upset when they hosted the Warriors the following week. It looked bad for Saudargas and company as the clock wound down, but last minute heroics by Johnny Wessels saved the Warriors from a Big Eight Conference loss that would have dropped them into a tie with the hotly pursuing Elgin Maroons, only one game behind the first place Warriors. The Cavalier's controlled the pace of the low-scoring game from the start, and the Warriors barely eked out an 8-7 lead in the first quarter. West held a 21-17 lead at halftime, but the Cavaliers outscored the Warriors in the third quarter to tie the game at 33. LaSalle-Peru surged ahead in the fourth quarter to take a 43-37 lead with four and half minutes left in the game. The gap was narrowed to two points when Gentry and Bobby Washington hit on free throws and Gentry scored on a tip-in. LaSalle-Peru then scored again and held a 45-41 lead with two minutes left, setting the stage for Wessels' dramatics. He scored on a tip-in and a free throw followed by a jump shot, then finished off his seven point surge with a layup just as the buzzer sounded. The 48-45 final score was the Warriors' narrowest victory margin of the season and marked the first time they were held below 50 points. Wessels had scored only eight points before his seven point surge in the last two minutes. His 15 point total was matched by Gentry, and Boshela added seven. Bobby Washington and Tom Olson were the only reserves to see action, sent in after both Parker and Boshela fouled out.

West breezed through the next three games, routing Sterling 93-55 in the final nonconference game of the season and winning high praise from veteran Sterling coach Gene Hall after the game: "Rockford West does everything well," he said. "It's the best high school team I've ever seen in all my years of coaching," In the conference games that followed, the Warriors topped Joliet 71-54, and beat Freeport 81-61 in a game with a combined total of 55 fouls. Gentry and Wessels fouled out, Boshela and Parker were called for four fouls each, and Coffman had three. Tom Olson came off the bench to fill in on the front line and chipped in eight points. Don Grabow sidelined by illness for nine games returned to action briefly when he came in at forward for a few minutes in the third quarter and for a little longer in the fourth.

Coach Saudargas and his Warriors were met by a very improved and very determined East Rockford quintet the next week when the E-Rabs hosted the Warriors for the final regular season game of the year. For the first time since the holiday break, East High coach Steve Polaski had his entire squad available without illness or injury, and his E-Rabs were eager to avenge their humiliating 69-25 loss to the Warriors at West earlier in the season. It was a taller and stronger E-Rab lineup, with Fred Clow, their 6'3" forward back in action after missing the first crosstown contest because of a leg injury. Joining the East squad since that game and adding height to the front line were 6'4" Joel Peterson and 6'3' Gary Lindsay. At center was 6'2" Tom Seger who had teamed up with 6'0" Joe Choppi to hold Wessels to just two points in the first game.

West won control of the ball at the tipoff, but lost possession when traveling was called. With the turnover, Polaski's E-Rabs revealed their game plan: keep the ball away from the Warriors' potent offense and force them to play defense the entire game. The E-Rabs controlled the ball for two and half minutes before the Warriors took it away and scored. Wessels hit from the field at that point and added two free throws to give West a 4-0 lead. East hit on its first five shots, including two free throws, and the game was tied at eight with two minutes left in the first quarter when Wessels gave the Warriors a 10-8 lead. Then Gentry caught fire and scored nine straight points, The Warriors led 32-19 at the half, but the E-Rabs fought back, outscoring West 14-7 in the third quarter and 12-10 in the fourth, keeping the outcome uncertain down to the wire. With two minutes left, East trailed by only four points, 43-39. A Gentry tip-in and two free throws by Fred Boshela made the margin 47-39, but East fought back again. Clow and Bob Lundquist hit to trim the lead to four, 47-43, but Coffman drove in for a layup to end the final E-Rab threat. Clow added two free throws at the buzzer, making the final 49-45.

For the third time in four years, Coach Saudargas and his Warriors were Big Eight Conference champs, but it took a perfect 10-0 record to edge out Elgin's Maroons. Their 9-1 record was marred only by their loss to the Warriors in the first conference game of the season. When postseason tournament pairings were announced by the Illinois High School Association, the two teams were in separate brackets, setting the stage for a rematch in Champaign if both teams managed to survive the challengers they faced along the way.

Coach Saudargas crowned his conference champion Warriors with cautious praise: "This year's team is the best I've ever had, but whether it's the best in the state remains to be seen. Don't forget that other favorites in the past were knocked off at tournament time. We haven't forgotten. In the 1951 state tourney, we saw Morton and La Grange — both unbeaten and both highly rated — fall on successive nights before a fired up Hinsdale team that had a mediocre season prior to its sensational upset victories. And last March, DuSable's fabulous Panthers, riding a 28 game victory streak, lost the biggest test of their prep careers when they fell before thrice-beaten Mount Vernon in the final game of the state tournament. Nothing is certain in Champaign."

Schools represented by teams in the state championship tournament at Champaign also were represented by Tournament Queen candidates. Carol Cleveland, seated second from the left, was chosen to represent West High School. Another candidate was named queen at the tournament won by the Warriors, but she and Warrior co-captain Rex Parker went on to graduate from Illinois State University together and were married.

No tomorrow

"Now it's one loss and you're out"
— Rockford Register-Republic Sports Editor Jim Johnston

Warriors Forever

Showtime

Coach Saudargas distraction-proofed his Warriors with his coaching strategy and with his own focused composure on the bench during even the most frenzied game situations. In the nerve-racking, cliffhanging tournament days ahead, that capacity for grace under pressure played as major a role in his personal life as it did in his Warriors' performance on the court.

While the Warriors, hundreds of sportswriters, thousands of other prep athletes throughout Illinois, and millions of basketball fans were focusing on March Madness, Coach Saudargas was ambushed by a personal crisis at home. His wife Alice was diagnosed with pregnancy toxemia (preeclampsia), a complication that threatens both the unborn child and the mother. Alice was in her eighth month, and her condition required constant medical monitoring.

"My blood pressure got so high the doctor put me on medication and ordered me to stay in bed" Alice said. "Alex just couldn't accept it when the doctor told us I wouldn't be able to go to the games, and he was bitterly, bitterly disappointed. I remember him saying, 'Who do you think I'm doing all this for?'"

Coach Saudargas handled his double load of stress at home and stress at work with his trademark calmness, and his Warriors helped by blowing away all three opponents in the Freeport Regional Tournament. They outscored their rivals 289 to 125 and set scoring records in the process: Lena fell to the Warriors 102-28 in the first round, with the West tally being the highest score in that regional's history and setting the Freeport high school gym record. Coffman was high scorer with 16, followed by Wessels and Gentry with 14 each. Warrior reserves accounted for 45 of West's points, led by Don Slaughter with 12 and Tom Olson with 10.

Those scoring records fell in the next game. The Warriors trounced Aquin of Freeport 111-42 in the semifinal. Coach Saudargas played his starters in the first and third quarters and his reserves in the second and fourth. Wessels led the scoring with 26 points, and junior reserve Slaughter came in behind Wessels with 16. Reserve Tom Olson, named to the Warriors' tournament roster for both his shooting skill and his flair for rousing esprit de corps, was lost for the postseason games with a knee injury near the end of the game.

"Olson never played regularly," Rod Coffman said, "but he was one of those guys you knew was always there for you. He didn't seem to care if he ever got into the game, just so we won. When one of us made a basket or a good play, he was the first one off the bench cheering. He never said a negative thing about any player or any play."

Coach Saudargas' oldest son Alex described Olson as a Warrior spark plug. "I always liked to see Olson come in," he said, "because when he got in, he was fired up. It was as though he thought, 'If I have this chance to play, I'm going to make the most of it.' He had a good jump shot. He could drive, then pull up and have a clear and easy shot while the guy guarding him was still backpedaling. He had that move, and he was a deadly free throw shooter."

Coach Saudargas moved Luther Bedford into Olson's spot on the roster for the regional championship game against Freeport. He used his entire 10-man squad in the game, and all 10 scored in the 76-55 win. Freeport tried to slow the action with a ball control game, but defensive work by Parker and Coffman in the backcourt foiled their strategy. The first quarter ended with West ahead 10-5, and the lead grew to 36-25 at the half. In the third quarter, the Warriors scored eight straight points before Freeport interrupted the run with two free throws, then West again poured in eight straight points. At the end of the third quarter, the Warriors led 61-32 and the Warrior reserves wrapped it up. Wessels led the starters with 23 points, Boshela 14, and Coffman 10. Washington led the reserves with nine points.

With the Freeport Regional Championship behind them, the Warriors returned home to host the Sectional Tournament, the last step before the state championship finals in Champaign. Other Regional Tournament winners advancing to the Sectional Tournament at West High were the Sycamore Spartans, East Rockford E-Rabs, and Rochelle Hubs. First round scheduling slated the Warriors against Rochelle and East Rockford against Sycamore, setting the scene for a potential Warriors versus E-Rabs Sectional Championship game.

It was not to be. Sycamore defeated East Rockford 74-66 in overtime while the Warriors rolled over Rochelle 84-67. Gentry led the way with one of his best nights in his prep career, scoring 28 points and turning in an outstanding defensive performance. Wessels added 16 points, Boshela 12, Parker seven, and Coffman six. Washington led the reserves with six points. Grabow and Slaughter added two each. Before the game, Coach Saudargas had tweaked his tournament roster by replacing 5'10" Bedford with 6'2" Joe DiGiovanni, adding more height and scoring power to the front line reserve. DiGiovanni responded by chipping in 5 points.

It was Wessels' turn to lead the assault the following night as the Warriors topped Sycamore for the Sectional Championship, 80-65. West jumped off to a 20-1 lead in the first quarter with what one sportswriter called "a machine-gun barrage of shots." Within 10 seconds of the opening tipoff, Gentry hit for two. Sycamore dumped in one free throw, then the Warriors scored 18 straight points in the next three minutes and 40 seconds: Wessels hit eight with an array of hook shots, jump shots, and layups. Coffman and Boshela added four each and Gentry two more.

Sycamore fought back in the second quarter after Gentry and Parker got into foul trouble and were taken out. The Spartans pumped in 17 points to the Warriors' six and closed the margin to 41-33 at the half. From that point on, the Warriors pulled away, outscoring the Spartans 25 to 10 in the third quarter. When the Warrior lead grew to 25 points, 70-45, early in the fourth quarter, Coach Saudargas emptied his bench. Wessels finished with 31 points, Boshela 16, Gentry 14, Coffman 10, and Parker seven.

Ear-splitting bedlam engulfed the West High gym for the last two and half minutes of the game as jubilant Warrior fans chanted "West High's going downstate!" over and over and over. At the final buzzer, the fans poured onto the court to embrace their Warrior heroes.

Well-wishing political and business leaders poured in congratulations after the Sectional Championship as sportswriters sized up the Warriors' chances against the other 15 sectional champions headed for the Sweet Sixteen finals in Champaign. But Coach Saudargas had more on his mind than the basketball powerhouses waiting to challenge his Warriors for the state crown. Alice was being told by her doctor that she could not accompany her husband to Champaign.

"My doctor told me I was in a really dangerous way medically and that I absolutely could not go to Champaign because something very serious could happen to me if I went," Alice said, "He even threatened not to be my doctor anymore if I wouldn't do what he told me to do.

"I argued with him because I knew Alex was so disappointed. I pointed out that two of his nurses were going to be at the games, so they could help if anything happened to me. He finally relented and said, 'I knew that you'd go even when I told you that you couldn't, but you have to promise that you'll go right to bed when you get down there and that you will stay in bed while you're at the hotel. When you go to the games, that's the only time you can get up and go out.' — which I agreed to do."

With matters settled on the home front, Coach Saudargas turned his attention to preparing his Warriors for their first challenger in Champaign, the Decatur Reds. Decatur had a taller front line than any other team the Warriors had faced all season and employed a run-and-shoot fast break offense. They were coached by future Illinois Basketball Coaches Association Hall-of-Famer Gay Kintner, who was returning to the state tournament for the eleventh time in his career. His Decatur Reds had won championships in 1931, 1936, and 1945.

Coach Saudargas cautioned that the opening round game would be one of his Warriors' roughest games of the season. "My boys are going to have the jitters," he said. "You don't just come down to Champaign for the first time and play your best the first time you go out on the court. Gay Kintner is a great coach, and he'll have his team as ready as they'll ever be."

What followed were days of high tension both on the court and off the court for both Alex and Alice.

Warriors Forever

All or nothing

"There was a lot expected of us from Rockford, from the people in the town, and I think it put a whole lot of pressure on us going into the state tournament. The one thing we didn't want to do was to come back here with anything but first place. It would have been a major, major disappointment to everyone here and to ourselves. We did not want to come back as anything but champions."

— *Rod Coffman, Warrior '55 starting guard*

Huff Gym at the University of Illinois in Champaign was more than twice as large as gyms where West High School and other tournament teams played regular season games — and so was the deafening roar from the crowd. Seating started right next to court boundary lines.

Cliffhangers and Nail-Biters

"I heard the clock strike 2:00 a.m." Nolden Gentry said about his restless night before the Warriors' first tournament game in Champaign. He was not alone.

"Everybody had the first game jitters," Coach Saudargas said. "I had them, too, but Gentry was the most jittery of all. We stopped in Normal just north of Bloomington en route from Rockford on Wednesday so our players could work out on the court at Illinois Normal University (now Illinois State University) before we continued on to Champaign. Gentry couldn't hit a thing at practice. He was fine the next day, game day, but all the others were tense then."

The intimidating expanse of the tournament arena at the University of Illinois dazzled the Warriors when they entered on Thursday. Gentry said, "Our first experience on the court in Champaign was when we warmed up to play Decatur. Huff Gym seated about 7,000 people. The gym at West High and other gyms where we played most of our games seated about 3,000, so it seemed like a mammoth place. It was a homey atmosphere because the seats were right on the out of bounds line, but it was the largest gym I had played in up to that time."

Not only were the Warriors playing before more than twice as many screaming fans packed into a gym more than twice the size of anything they had experienced before, they also were the center of attention for a flurry of media cameras and microphones. In addition to the usual play-by-play of their court action by sportscaster Morey Owens to home town fans on Rockford's WROK, other broadcasters were describing the action to millions of basketball fans throughout the state.

Beyond traditional radio and print media attention, the 1955 games featured a state tournament first: live telecasts of the finals to homes throughout Illinois and beyond, reaching what at that time was the tournament's largest audience ever. TV sportscaster Jack Drees, the voice of nationally televised Pabst Blue Ribbon boxing bouts and of college and NFL football games, was joined as host for the telecast by "Chick" Hearn, later the voice of the Los Angeles Lakers. Hearn's rapid fire, staccato

WROK sportscaster Morey Owens was the voice of the Warriors.

style descriptions and colorful phrasing made popular such basketball terms as "slam dunk," "air ball," and "no harm-no foul."

The Decatur-Rockford matchup was a tournament centerpiece because the Warriors were rated number one in the state by the final Associated Press and United Press International polls and because jitters-plagued games in opening rounds were notorious for producing upsets. Media billing touted the game as the battle of the giants, with five of the ten starters for Rockford and Decatur towering to 6'5" or above. Visiting coaches whose teams had been eliminated in regional and sectional play were astonished at the size of the combatants. Mt. Carmel coach Roy Gatewood, a University of Illinois Basketball Hall-of-Famer credited with originating the jump shot as a 1946-49 Illini forward said, "I've never seen such big teams. I'd be ashamed to bring my little kids up to this tournament." Danville coach Art Mathison, captain and center for the University of Illinois team that won the Big Ten Conference co-championship in the war-shortened 1943 season, told reporters, "I'd be just another sub on that West squad."

Within minutes of the opening tipoff, the game showed signs of an upset in the making. Gentry and Wessels scored the first six points, but Decatur bounced back with ten in a row. Then Wessels drove in for a layup and added two free throws to end the first quarter with the score knotted at 10.

A seesaw battle ensued in the second quarter with the lead changing hands four times before the Warriors surged ahead 27-18, the largest lead either team held in the game. Decatur fought back to score eight straight points in the last two minutes, cutting the Warriors' lead to one point, 27-26, at the half.

The heated pace continued in the second half with the scored tied seven times and the lead changing hands seven times. By the end of the third quarter, Decatur had forged ahead 42-40.

At that point, Coach Saudargas abandoned his zone defense and ordered his Warriors into a full-court press. Boshela tied the game at 42-42, then fouled out and was replaced by Grabow. Decatur went ahead 44-42, but Coffman tied it at 44-44. Again Decatur went ahead 46-44, and again Coffman tied it 46-46.

With about two minutes left on the clock and Decatur leading 49-48, Coffman hit a 15 foot jump shot to give the Warriors the lead. Gentry followed it with a layup. As the clock ticked past the one minute mark with the Warriors holding a two point lead, Gentry blocked a Decatur corner shot and the Warriors took possession. Coffman and Gentry scored again, making it ten points in the last two minutes for the Coffman-Gentry duo, and the Warriors held on to win 58-54.

Decatur coach Kintner said after the game that Gentry's defensive play gave West the victory: "The turning point was that blocked corner shot at the end of the game," he said. "Gentry slapped it down in the air. That shot would've tied up the game for us, but instead West got the ball."

Gentry led Warrior scoring with 21 points and bolstered the Warriors' effort with strong rebounding and defense, blocking several Decatur shots in addition to the critical blocked shot in the final minute. Wessels added 15 points but was off his game, hitting on only five of 24 shots from the floor. Coffman chipped in 12, with eight of them coming in the fourth quarter when he scored half of the Warriors' 16 points. Boshela added six before fouling out in the fourth quarter, and his replacement, Grabow, added four.

As the happy Warriors filed into their locker room, Coach Saudargas told reporters, "I wasn't surprised a bit at how close it was. We knew all along they were rough — as good as Elgin or any other team we've played all season. The worst part is always that first game. We'll play better tomorrow."

Gentry seconded the motion: "It was just a case of butterflies today. Tomorrow we'll really go. Now that this one is over, I can get some sleep."

But back in Rockford, sleep was the last thing on anyone's mind. The Warriors' game had been broadcast into West High classrooms, and the victory brought pandemonium. Students burst from classrooms as the school song blared through the hallways. The band played on as lockers were opened, emptied, and slammed shut by students racing to the parking lot and cramming into cars. Classes were the last thing on their minds, and many students decided school was out for the duration of the tournament, with or without the permission of Principal James Blue. Warrior fever gripped students and faculty alike, and the infection spread to everyone everywhere in Rockford, border to border.

Rested and confident after surviving Thursday's battle royal with Decatur, the Warriors found time for some pressure-relieving hijinks. "Rex Parker was seen walking on his hands down the hall of the Inman Hotel," a school newspaper staffer reported. "It was only to win a bet from a Shawneetown (lost to Princeton in the second round) supporter that he could walk upside down longer than the 'Southerner' could." Parker said Wessels had his own diversion. "We were on the fourth or fifth floor of the Inman, and Johnny would open the window anytime anyone was down below and yell, 'Okay, let's get behind the mighty Warriors!' I don't know how many times he did that during the time we were down there."

Warrior fever intensified Friday afternoon as the Warriors moved one step closer to the coveted state championship, coasting to an easy victory over the Lincoln Railsplitters, 75-65, but not before some anxious moments for Coach Saudargas. When it came time to go over the game plan and give each player specific instructions, Wessels was missing.

Nobody knew where he was, but one of the assistant coaches said he knew Wessels was in the gym because he rode from the hotel with him.

With Wessels missing, Coach Saudargas told Grabow he would start and gave him the instructions meant for Wessels. While the Warriors were warming up, Wessels came running down an aisle and into the Warrior dressing room. When he reached the floor and started warming up, Coach Saudargas asked him where he had been. Wessels explained that he had a date with an East High cheerleader and had to get her a ticket.

With Wessels starting at center, West jumped off to a 15-5 lead in the first quarter and expanded it to 38-13 at the half. In the second half, Coach Saudargas began experimenting with his lineup and resting some of his players with an eye towards Saturday's two finals. "Our boys are strong and like to play," he said, "but playing two games in one day can hurt anyone, especially when they're playing under such pressure.

"We could have scored more points if I had left the first team in and stuck with our usual style of offense, but I wanted to try some different offenses and new defenses. We were hurting on fouls, too, so we didn't do too much guarding under the basket.

"Our kids were more relaxed and moved better today," he said. "Wessels was shooting better and we got some good scoring out of our guards, too."

The guards combined to pour in 20 points: Coffman 11, Parker 7, and Washington added 2 after Coffman fouled out. Gentry led the team with 20 points. Wessels added 18, and Boshela 12.

At the end of the day, only four of the 16 teams that traveled to Champaign were still standing, and three of the four teams were from northern Illinois: Princeton, Elgin, and Rockford West. The lone southern team was Pinckneyville, the perennial powerhouse slated to play the Warriors in the semi-finals Saturday afternoon.

Pinckneyville had replaced the Warriors as the number one team in the Associated Press poll for three weeks after the Warriors lost to Rock Island, and Coach Saudargas said the Warriors were fired up for the game. "All season the kids have been saying, 'We'd sure like to have a chance to play them.'"

Elgin's Maroons were saying the same thing about playing the Warriors again to avenge their defeat by West in the first conference game of the season. The Maroons' loss gave the Warriors the Big Eight Conference championship and left Elgin in second place.

Warrior wishes for a head-on encounter with Pinkneyille were coming true Saturday. Elgin's hopes for a second match with the Warriors hinged on the outcome of the Rockford-Pinckneyville and Elgin-Princeton semifinal games Saturday afternoon.

The showdown would follow in the championship battle Saturday night — a history-making thriller featuring what a veteran Chicago sportswriter described as the most incredible miracle-moment in sports.

Opposites clash . . .

"When the West Rockford Warriors meet the Pinckneyville Panthers, it will be a battle between the champions of two extremely different styles of basketball."
— *Illinois sportswriter Mark Novak*

Warriors Forever

Living in Day-Tight Compartments . . .

Coach Saudargas had a lot on his mind when Saturday dawned. He and his Warriors were coming up against a living legend, Coach Duster Thomas, Pinckneyville's wonder worker who specialized in toppling towering teams like the Warriors. Next up only hours later — if the Warriors survived Pinckneyville — would be the championship game against the winner of the Elgin vs. Princeton contest. Both were powerful teams, and each posed radically different coaching challenges. All the while, Coach Saudargas was carrying an extra but hidden weight of worry about his ailing wife. Alice had traveled to Champaign-Urbana to be with her husband for the championship games despite her frail health and difficult pregnancy. Both she and Alex knew the impending birth of their child could happen at any moment.

With his inveterate calm and laser focus, Coach Saudargas concentrated on each challenge as it came, starting with plans for thwarting the strategy Coach Thomas and his Pinckneyville Panthers had used successfully against other highly ranked powerhouses, Centralia and Colllinsville, in earlier action and against Alton and Quincy in the state finals. Coach Thomas cut taller teams down to size with a slow, methodical, ball-control offense while his Panthers induced opponents' key players to foul out. The strategy provided a twofold payoff for the Panthers. First, their 82 percent free throw accuracy padded the Panthers' scoring tally and balanced or overcame any advantage opponents had in hitting from the floor. Second, when opponents' key players fouled out, their coaches were forced to compromise original game plans and improvise with less skillful substitutes.

Coach Saudargas decided to counter the Pinckneyville strategy by using a zone defense and calling off his Warriors' usual attack-dog offense. "We had one thing in mind," he told reporters later, "and that was not to foul. We knew if we did, Pinckneyville would keep sinking those free throws. I planned several defenses, but I thought the best way to play the Pincks was to play a slow game along with them." He said he knew he could use the Warriors' height advantage to control rebounding and could rely on high percentage shots from the floor to outscore the Panthers, "but I didn't want to try to match them at the free throw line."

His plan worked despite a first quarter flourish by Pinckneyville giving the Panthers an 11-8 lead at the end of the quarter. The lead changed hands several time in the second quarter before the Warriors scored six straight points in the last 90 seconds to wipe out a Panther 21-20 lead and wrap up the first half leading 26-21. The Warriors never trailed again.

Coach Saudargas bolstered his game plan with a late second quarter position change that paid off in the second half. He switched Johnny Wessels from center to forward and replaced him with Fred Boshela at the pivot post. Pinckneyville defenders had trouble covering Boshela, and he responded with eight baskets and five free throws, including four straight baskets in the third quarter that twice put the Warriors ahead by seven. The third quarter ended with the Warriors leading 42-35.

Pinckneyville battled back in the fourth quarter, narrowing the Warriors' lead to two points, 42-40, with 5:29 to go. Then Coffman dropped in a layup to make it 44-40. Pinckneyville responded with a full court press, but deft moves by Parker and Coffman outran the Panthers. Parker added two more free throws and Wessels a layup to boost the West lead to 10 points, 50-40 with 1:52 left on the clock. The Panthers staged a last-minute rally with two baskets and two free throws, but the rally fizzled when Gentry countered with a layup and Boshela added a tip-in.

The Warriors finished their 54-46 win with a .571 shooting percentage, hitting on 20 of 35 shots, the best recorded by any team in the tournament. Gentry was perfect at four for four and Boshela followed up with eight for 11. Boshela was high scorer for both teams with 21 points. Wessels added 14 before fouling out in the fourth quarter, Gentry nine, Coffman six, and Parker four.

Sportswriters heaped high praise on Coach Saudargas in postgame analyses. "Veteran writers from Champaign and Chicago agreed readily that Alex had put forth one of the top coaching efforts in recent years," Rockford sportswriter Jim Johnston said. "His strategy, both planned and on-the-spot varieties, was great. The Warriors knew just what to do and did it well. Duster pulled his ace out of the sleeve early when he tried his 4-1 'T-formation' offense which is supposed to drive any defense frantic, but Alex and the kids were ready for it and it never had a chance. The Warriors played to avoid mistakes. They did. They played to control the boards. They did."

Coach Saudargas also thwarted Pinckneyville's foul-inducing strategy with his "do not foul" warning to his players and by moving Wessels out of the hoop area where many fouls are called. The move kept Wessels in the game till he finally fouled out in the fourth quarter. Gentry was in foul trouble late in the game with four fouls, but Rex Parker, who had fouled out of three regular season games, had no fouls called on him.

The victory brought new challenges for Coach Saudargas. Elgin triumphed over Princeton in their semifinal match, setting the scene for the first and only Illinois State Basketball Championship matchup between two Big Eight Conference teams. Within a few hours, his Warriors would face a team that played a very different style of basketball —and a team hungry to avenge their loss to the Warriors in the first conference game of the season.

With Alice back at the Inman Hotel recouping her strength before the championship game, Coach Saudargas reviewed and updated the game plan he had used successfully against Elgin earlier. He knew it was not the same team the Warriors had defeated then; it was now a highly motivated team with something to prove, a score to settle. He was also aware of another potential peril his jubilant Warriors faced after defeating Pinckneyville. Rex Parker pinpointed the peril later: "A lot of us thought that if we could beat Pinckneyville, we could win the state. From the time we were in the eighth or ninth grade, we always saw Pinckneyville and Taylorville and Centralia as leaders in the southern Illinois area known as "Little Egypt" which produced so many championship teams. When we beat them, it may have made us a little overconfident. We thought, 'Well, we beat Pinckneyville and we already beat Elgin in Big Eight Conference play, so we shouldn't have any problems.'"

Rod Coffman, Parker's counterpart at guard, expressed the same confidence, and was as focused on the night's TV coverage as he was on the looming battle with Elgin. "Between the semifinal game when we beat Pinckneyville and the final game against Elgin, I thought I should get a haircut because it was going to be the biggest game of my life. I was going to be playing before I don't know how many people, and the TV stations were going to broadcast it all over the state. My grandmother and grandfather were going to be watching, and I wanted to make sure I looked decent. I thought my hair was too long, so I told the coaches I was going to get a haircut at the hotel barbershop. The coaches got on my back and said, 'Absolutely not.' We were supposed to be resting up for the Elgin game, so I had to abandon the idea."

Warrior overconfidence was about to be shattered by a humiliating drubbing in front of their TV audience and thousands of anguished Warrior fans packed to the rafters in Huff Gym.

The agony and the ecstasy

"Anything can happen in Champaign."
— Coach Saudargas

Warriors Forever

"What Am I Doing Down Here?"

Sportswriters billed Saturday night's game as "the battle in the valley of the giants," featuring the two tallest state championship finalists in the tournament's 48-year history. Elgin averaged 6'3 1/2" and Rockford 6'4". But even the sportswriters' most impassioned buildups for the championship matchup fell short of the hold-your-breath, edge-of-your-seat drama that followed.

Not all the drama was in the media spotlight. As Coach Saudargas warmed up his Warriors for the last stretch in their climb to the coveted summit of Illinois prep basketball, Alice climbed the bleachers to her seat and joined the Rockford throng to cheer on her husband and their hometown favorites. But she had more on her mind than basketball. "I started feeling labor pains coming on at the hotel," she said, "but they weren't too close together, about every two or three hours, so I wasn't worried. And as I climbed up the stands, I saw my doctor's nurses already there. I knew they would be able to help me in a crisis."

Across the gym, a living icon of Sweet Sixteen basketball tournaments was facing a modest crisis of his own. Jack Flannery, later inducted into the Illinois Basketball Hall of Fame as a faithful fan, had attended every state tournament for 42 years and always rooted for any team from northern Illinois. He was a graduate of the old Rockford High School before it was replaced by East High and West High, but had settled in Aurora, about 70 miles southeast of Rockford and only 25 miles south of Elgin. Flannery often sat with the cheerleaders and was regarded by some as a sort of good luck charm. Because both Elgin's Maroons and Rockford's Warriors were from northern Illinois, he was in a quandary about which team to cheer for in the championship game. Finally Flannery made what later appeared to be a fateful decision, cheering for the Maroons in the first half and for the Warriors in the second half.

Meanwhile back in Rockford, the championship game had transformed the bustling metropolis into what looked like an eerie, desolate ghost town. Rod Coffman said his brother went out to pick up a pizza just before the game and found the streets of the city completely deserted. Everyone was huddled around their TVs or radios in anticipation.

Coach Saudargas' son Alex said there was as much excitement outside Huff gym as there was inside. "People were everywhere scalping tickets and trying to buy tickets," he said. "It was amazing. I remember getting separated from my brother in the crowd as we were walking to the gym and hearing some guy call me over. 'Hey, kid,' he said, 'I'll give you 25 bucks for your ticket.' In 1955, that was a lot of money. Let me tell you, I gave it some thought. By the time I got inside, it was standing room only and everybody was so keyed up you could feel the tension."

But the tension in the arena did not extend into the Warriors' locker room. So confident were the Warriors before taking the court that co-captains Parker and Coffman conspired for a little horseplay. "We were the ones who always led the team out on the floor," Coffman said, "but Don Grabow didn't care if we were co-captains or not, and he loved to lead the team out. He would always edge his way to the front and try to be the first one out of the locker room to run onto the floor. So on the way up the steps, Don was nudging his way to the front. Rex and I said, 'Let's let him go. Let's keep the team behind us and let him go out on the floor by himself.' At the entryway into the gym, we all stood back while Don took off down the floor, dribbling like crazy. When he got to the basket and realized he was all by himself, he turned around and said, 'Come on, you guys, come on!'"

Warming up on the other end of the court were Elgin's resolute Maroons, preparing to take the Warriors' high spirits down a peg and give their overweening self-assurance a severe jolt. While the Warriors had a relatively easy time of it against Pinkneyville in the afternoon game, Elgin had fought from behind to overcome Princeton in their semifinal match with heroics by 5'11 guard Paul Hudgens. He scored 22 points in the afternoon semifinal, including five straight baskets and a free throw for 11 points in just over two minutes of the fourth quarter to lead his Maroons to victory. He was helped in the cause with 19 points by center Tom Aley and with 14 points from playmaker-guard Gary "Whitey" Smith, a deadly outside shooter and one of the tournament's top scorers.

West High grabbed the opening tipoff, but a wild shot from the corner by Wessels bounced off the side of the backboard and went out of bounds, an ill omen of what was to follow for the Warriors' leading scorer. Elgin fared no better when it took possession, missing their first two shots and a free throw. The Maroons finally opened the scoring only to be matched by the Warriors seconds later. From that point on, the lead changed hands five times during the first four minutes, until Elgin pulled ahead 8 to 7.

Warrior fans had little to cheer about for the rest of the first half. The Maroons took charge and nearly ran the Warriors off the court. Suddenly the Warriors seemed to be a different team, lackadaisical, flubbing passes, missing free throws, blowing easy shots, and fouling repeatedly. Elgin increased its lead steadily for the next four minutes, leading 24-10 at the end of the first quarter, and increasing their lead to 16 points, 26-10, in the first minutes of the second quarter.

At that point, Coach Saudargas called for a full-court press to stem the Maroon's onslaught. It worked for a few minutes. The Warriors scored eight straight points on baskets by Boshela, Coffman, and Parker to narrow the Maroon's lead to 26-18 with four minutes to go in the half. Then Elgin regained its momentum and outscored the Warriors 14 to 9 in the remaining minutes. Coach Saudargas sent Grabow in for the badly faltering Wessels and, with both his guards having four fouls on them, he substituted Bobby Washington for Rex Parker. The half ended with the Maroons on top by 13 points, 40-27.

West High fans cheered the Warriors on, but it wasn't looking good for their favorites when the first half ended.

"It was a disastrous first half," Alice said. "On our side of the gym, there was just gloom and doom. Everyone felt so depressed we just wanted to sit and cry. When we went out to go to the bathroom or whatever during halftime, none of us were in a rush to get back. Huff Gym had just one women's bathroom, and it was up on the second floor. By the time I got there, a long line had formed, but I didn't care. I waited in line and just took my time. I was asking myself, 'Do I want to go back in there and watch them get really beat, or not?'"

Saudargas' son Alex, who was in the stands with his brother Richard and sister Christine, said, "At the half, all the fans around us were saying, 'Poor West. Well, at least they made it to the finals.' I think everybody was searching for some sort of solace in that because things looked so bad. Everyone was resigned to West losing — everyone except my father. He had no intention of losing that game."

"It was quiet in our locker room," Coffman said. "Coach was very calm, but he wasn't the type who would yell and scream anyway. We could hear them in the Elgin locker room which was right next door. They were going crazy, yelling and screaming. Somebody said he heard Coach Chesbrough telling his players they were the new state champions."

Bobby Washington said there was a feeling of disbelief in the Warrior locker room. "When you're used to winning, it's almost like you can't believe it when you don't," he said. "It's like a boxer, undefeated, who gets hit and knocked down, and asks himself, 'What am I doing down here?' It's that kind of mentality. You know you have to keep coming back; just do what you're supposed to do and you'll be fine. Coach Saudargas was cool and calm, but hearing them whoop up next door and saying we were dead and buried kind of inspired us a little."

Don Krieschbaum, who coached the Warriors their sophomore year, said Coach Saudargas knew how coaches' behavior in certain situations affects the players. "He was easy going, a good psychologist, and he knew his players well. In the locker room, Alex didn't say much. He told them, 'Listen to them. They think they've got you beat.' I think he felt that was enough to say."

Saudargas' son Richard, later a Tennessee University psychology professor, agreed: "My father used a problem-solving approach as a coach," he said. "That means saying, 'Look, we're in this situation; now, what do we have to do to get out of it? I'm going to show you what you need to do to solve the problem.' It's a matter of not panicking and of just going ahead and doing your job. It's more effective than any emotional, rah-rah approach. He believed the typical rah-rah business was overrated."

Coach Saudargas later confirmed his son's assessment in an interview with Rockford Register Star reporter Mike Doyle: "At half-time, I told the kids, 'We've tried everything and nothing is working. Now we're going to try something new. We'll play man-to-man, and maybe we can surprise them."

"We talked more strategy than anything else during halftime" Coffman said. "The biggest change was that we were going to go into a man-to-man, full court press starting the third quarter even though Rex and I had four fouls on us."

Krieschbaum said . "It took a lot of courage to go into a full-court press when both starting guards had four fouls. I was surprised he did that, and so was the other coach. If you were sitting in the stands watching that, you'd think, 'O good Lord, what's he doing?' But he always had things like that going on in his mind, catching the other team by surprise."

What followed in the second half surprised not only Elgin's Maroons, but also everyone in Huff Gym and in the radio/TV audience throughout the entire state.

Complete bedlam

"It seems funny in a way that a gym seating only 7,000 persons can create so much more furor on a basketball Saturday night than a stadium seating nearly 10 times that many can create on a football Saturday afternoon in the fall."
— *Rockford Register-Republic Sports Editor Jim Johnston*

With the clock running out and the championship on the line, the Warriors gather to plan and refocus one last time. Wessels, left, reflects the game pressure as he glances across the court. With him, left to right, are Coffman, Coach Saudargas, Gentry, Boshela, and Parker. "We said a prayer before breaking up the huddle," Parker said, "not for victory, but for strength to play to the best of our ability to the end."

It's Not Over Till It's Over.

As the halftime break ended, Coffman had more on his mind than the full court press. "I was thinking, 'No, we cannot let this happen. We cannot lose this game.' The one thing I knew was that if we went home with anything but first place, it was going to be a major, major disappointment in Rockford. When I thought about facing my brothers and friends of my brothers, my friends, family and then a zilllion other people, I didn't want to face those people and have to say, 'At least we won second place.' I'm telling you, I was frightened. I thought, 'If we're going to lose, I'm going to go down trying.' Johnny Wessels was usually our leading scorer, but he was having a terrible game. I decided I had to make a greater contribution."

Elgin had shut down Wessels completely in the first half with brutal defense. Coach Saudargas' son Alex said, "They were muscling him and getting away with all kinds of rough stuff. He got an elbow in the nose and he got an elbow in the chest. He took some vicious hits. I kept watching that and getting frustrated when none of it was called." Wessels' sister, Mary Creagan, said she and their mother saw that he was bleeding and were so worried they went down at halftime to see if he was okay.

With Wessels hobbled and off his game, Coffman resolved to fill the void: "I took it upon myself to start shooting more."

Before heading out for the second half, Gentry called his teammates together for a prayer to play well. When they emerged from the locker room and ran up the steps into the arena, they were greeted by the rousing sound of "Rock Around The Clock," blaring from Huff Gym's public address system. Tom Olson's mother had gone out during halftime for a 45 rpm copy of the rock and roll hit by Bill Haley & His Comets and arranged for it to be played as the Warriors returned to action.

Coffman acted immediately on his resolve. The Warriors grabbed the third period tip-off and Coffman sank a shot from 20 feet out the first time he got his hands on the ball. The Warriors' man-to-man full-court press rattled Elgin. They responded with a pass over the top of Warrior defenders and scored about one minute into the quarter. That was the Maroon's last basket for nearly four minutes. Stealing the ball and running fast breaks, the Warriors poured in 10 straight points, including another basket and two free throws by Coffman, two baskets by Wessels and one free throw each by Boshela and Gentry to get back in the game, closing the Elgin lead to 42-39.

"What helped us a lot," Coffman said, "was that Elgin decided the way to beat the press was to throw long passes instead of dribbling the ball upcourt. That was not very good strategy on their part because if Rex and I were forced to guard closely anybody bringing the ball up, our chances of drawing a foul would have been much greater. When they started throwing long passes, it took us out of the play for a while."

Meanwhile, Alice and others who had left the gym depressed after the Warriors disastrous first half had straggled back to the gym entry but were locked out. "They wouldn't let anybody in," she said. "We could hear all the screaming and yelling and clapping and wanted to get in there to see what was going on. Finally we were let in during a time out and I saw that we were really coming back. The score was almost tied and it was turning into an exciting game."

It was too exciting for Rod Coffman's brother back in Rockford. "I had one brother who was trying to watch the game on TV," Coffman said, "but he was so nervous he thought he was going to have a heart attack. He left the room when he couldn't take it anymore. His wife would come in and give him a blow by blow report of what was happening on TV."

Elgin scored again with about three minutes remaining in the quarter, but Coffman dropped in two more baskets in a row, bringing the Warriors to within one point of Elgin, 44-43. Moments later Parker added two free throws to put the Warriors ahead for the first time since the opening minutes of the game.

Elgin's "Whitey" Smith sank a jump shot to put Elgin ahead again 46-45 as the quarter wound down. Parker tied the game at 46 with another free throw, but Smith again put Elgin ahead 48-46. Then Coffman added a free throw and the quarter ended with the Maroon's on top 48-47.

West High took the lead 49-48 at the start of the fourth quarter when Boshela pumped in a jump shot. Elgin's Gary Seigmeier followed with three free throws after being fouled twice, giving Elgin a 51-49 advantage. At the halfway point of the quarter Boshela tied the score again with two free throws.

West's comeback hopes were dashed during the next two minutes when Elgin's star-shooters from the outside took charge. Paul Hudgens sank a jump shot and "Whitey" Smith followed suit. Then Hudgens scored again on a steal and easy layup giving the Maroons a commanding 57-51 lead with just 2:19 to go.

Chicago American sportswriter Bill Gleason said his Chicago Tribune counterpart Charlie Bartlett told him at that point, "Elgin deserves it. It's Chesbrough's turn tonight."

Warrior-backer Mary Lou Yankaitis and others in Huff Gym and in the radio-TV audience agreed with Bartlett's verdict. Mary Lou, West High's bookkeeper, and her husband thought Elgin's six point lead meant that the game was over, so they decided to leave. "We wanted to beat the traffic," she said. "After we got into the car and headed north, we turned on the radio and were shocked to hear that the game was tied."

Gleason, later inducted into the Illinois Basketball Hall of Fame as a journalist and writing for the Chicago Sun-Times, cited what happened next as the most memorable moment in any sports event he ever covered, transcending anything in the NFL, including Super Bowl games, major league baseball regular season and World Series games, or any other amateur, college, or professional sports event.

With 2:19 on the clock, Gleason wrote, "West Rockford forward Nolden Gentry went up for a shot. Foul! After the shot, a referee ruled. (Continuous action was not a factor then.) Gentry got a free throw and a chance for a bonus throw. He made both. A four point play.

"Elgin put the ball in play. West Rockford's Parker went for a steal. Collision. Whistle. Saudargas grimaced on the bench. He couldn't lose Parker. The call went against Elgin forward Gary Seigmeier. It was his fifth, and he would be the only player to foul out of this wild game.

"Parker, who had been cold from the field, rolled in both free throws. 'Check the clock,' Bartlett shouted through the din. 'One second. Six points in one second.'"

The scoreboard read 57-57 with 2:18 left. Forty-five seconds later Boshela put the Warriors ahead 59-57, only to have Smith tie the game again with 1:15 to play. West appeared to regain the lead when Boshela drove in for a layup with 46 seconds to go, but he was called for charging Elgin defender Earl Lamp and the basket was disallowed. Lamp's free throw attempt bounced around the rim twice, then bounced out and Wessels came down with the rebound.

Coach Saudargas called a time out and gathered his players to discuss a plan. The goal was to get the ball to Wessels for a last second shot, Coffman said. "Even though he was having a bad game, he was our best shooter and leading scorer all season." Wessels had hit on only two of 13 shots attempted in the game, far below his normal forty percent average. "We planned for him to shoot," Gentry said, "because we just didn't feel he could continue missing, as good a shooter as he was."

After the time out, Coffman received the throw in from Parker. "We got the ball to Wessels," Coffman said, "but instead of tossing it back out, he shot too soon, while there were still 16 seconds left."

The ball bounced off the back of the hoop and out toward the free throw circle, but Gentry was there to follow up Wessels' shot. "My man didn't block me off the boards," Gentry said, "so I had an open track to the basket."

Gentry seemed to come out of nowhere, West High sportswriter Dick Lundeen said, "leaping high and tipping the sphere back through the hoop." The Warriors led 61-59.

With only about 10 seconds left, "Whitey" Smith, Elgin's most dangerous shooter and a star player for the Maroons all season, brought the ball down the court. "It was my job to guard him," Coffman said. "I was staying close to him and was going to let him take a flyer, one of those really long shots if he wanted to, but I wasn't going to let him get anywhere near the basket.

"As he moved down, I had the feeling he was taking way too long. With about 8 seconds to go, I was ticking down to myself, six, five, four, and then I knew he had lost track of how much time was left. Everyone was yelling at him and the place was going crazy, fans were going crazy, so he couldn't hear his coach, he couldn't hear his teammates yelling for him to shoot or anything, and by the time he realized what was happening, it was too late to take a shot."

Pandemonium followed. Elgin collapsed in grief and tears. Wessels fainted and had to be helped off the floor. Warrior fans in ecstatic jubilation and euphoria overwhelmed security and rushed onto the floor to hug their new state champions. It took more than a half hour to restore order so trophies could be presented to the teams. And it took another half hour before the triumphant Warriors were able to work their way to their dressing room.

Cheerleader Sue Swanson and Warrior reserve Don Grabow embrace while starting forward Fred Boshela, 53, is caught up in the wave of ecstatic fans.

Meanwhile in Rockford, West High fans poured out of their homes shouting spontaneous cheers for their Warriors. Others piled into cars decorated with streaming banners and school colors and drove through downtown Rockford, filling city streets with the sounds of blaring horns and cries of joy into the early morning hours.

Sportswriters filed stirring stories of unparalleled, unsurpassed, and impassioned tourney drama featured on front pages of Sunday morning newspapers in Rockford and throughout the state.

"West Rockford's Warriors staged one of the most dramatic comebacks and most hair-raising windups in the history of Illinois state prep basketball tournaments," Rockford sportswriter Jim Johnston reported. "It undoubtedly will be recorded as the greatest comeback in Sweet 16 history."

Bloomington sportswriter Fred Young said, "It was as stirring a battle as had ever been witnessed in George Huff Gymnasium." And Champaign sportswriter Ron Lawfer told readers, "A storybook finish for the Illinois State High School tournament wrapped up at exactly 10:24 p.m. Saturday, and all the tension and emotion that had been stored up for an entire season broke loose."

Atop the Huff Gym scoreboard at one end of the court where history had just been made was an Illinois map with lights for each of the sixteen cities represented in the tournament. Only two

lights were left burning when Elgin's Maroons and Rockford's Warriors took to the court for the Sweet 16 grand finale. Now only the Rockford light was burning. West High School was the 1955 Illinois State Basketball Champion.

"The greatest salute ever"

"Veteran Sweet Sixteen observers said what followed West High School's state championship was 'the greatest salute to a prep champion ever.'"
— *Pete Turco, Chicago Daily News*

"One more thing: Saudargas' wife, Alice, mother of nine, was extremely pregnant. She was expected to deliver their tenth child momentarily, like during the six-point rally or in the victory caravan back to Rockford. Loyal fan that she was, Alice did not upstage the tumultuous welcome for the team."
— *Bill Gleason, Chicago American*

Glory Days

Warrior fever grew even more impassioned in Rockford Sunday morning as thousands prepared to welcome their triumphant heroes home. Many decided not to wait; a steady stream of cars packed with rabid Warrior rooters headed south from Rockford to meet up with the team on the highway traveling north.

"Everyone was so excited after the game it was hard to sleep Saturday night," Alice said. "Mayor Milton Lundstrom and others had scheduled a celebration for 6 p.m. at West High, so we got together for breakfast and planned for the trip home. It was a drizzly, cold, nasty day, and the trip was going to take about five and a half hours. My pains had been coming more often, so it was decided that the children and I would ride in a car with Tommy Olson's parents, following the others in case we couldn't make it to the school."

As they packed their bags, they anticipated the celebration in the West High gym. What no one anticipated was the unprecedented, jaw-dropping fervor they would meet on the road or the frenzied throng waiting to swallow up the Warriors when they arrived in Rockford.

Rockford police officer Earl Sudduth, a former Golden Gloves boxing champion who was assigned to accompany the team to Champaign, organized the ten car victory caravan outside the Inman Hotel. Sportswriters from Chicago and Rockford rode with Sudduth to chronicle the trip home. After a slight delay because Nolden Gentry couldn't find his luggage, the caravan left the Inman for Rockford about 11:30.

Because there were no high school sub-classifications or separate tournaments for each class in Illinois then, there was only one state tournament with only one state champion, and the whole state, north and south, east and west, knew who it was. All along the way on the road home the Warriors were greeted with waves and cheers.

At Bloomington, about an hour north and west of Champaign, the caravan was slowed by city traffic. As the cars were refueled, Sudduth called for help. He contacted Bloomington police, who provided an escort with flashing lights through the city and radioed ahead to other cities along the caravan's route. Ten more carloads of Warrior fans joined the caravan in Bloomington.

Illinois State Police took up the escort for a short distance at El Paso about 15 miles north of Bloomington. "The caravan passed through each town with horns blaring," Rockford sportswriter Jim Johnston wrote. "We knew we were back in Big Eight territory when we reached LaSalle, about 70 miles south of Rockford. LaSalle police picked up the caravan on the outskirts and escorted it through the city while the citizenry gave recognition with waves of congratulations and cheers."

Three hours into the trip, Coach Saudargas and Alice had some anxious moments when the caravan pulled off the highway for lunch in Mendota. After lunch and a photo session with Mendota newspaper reporters, the caravan prepared to resume its northward journey. Departure was delayed when Olson's car with Alice aboard had a flat tire. "They were very nervous about me and my labor pains, of course," Alice said. "They were afraid I was going to have the baby right in the car." Johnston said the crisis was resolved when "a borrowed tire was put in place so the Olsons and Saudargases could rejoin the caravan for the victory parade. Half an hour or so later the Warrior caravan was on its way again with Mendota police escorting it through the city and citizens cheering as the

Warriors went by." More carloads of fans joined the parade in Mendota and steady rain began to fall as the parade moved north.

A permanent state police escort picked up the caravan at the junction of highways 51 and 30 about 37 miles south of Rockford. Chicago American sportswriter Bill Gleason said, "Between that intersection and Rochelle 25 miles south of Rockford the parade was doubled and tripled time after time. Loyal Rockfordites were parked in every farmer's driveway and every side road that led onto the highway waiting to join the procession.

"When the parade reached the junction of highways 64 and 51, approximately 50 more cars were waiting in restaurant parking lots. It went on like this for miles."

At that point, Chicago Daily News sportswriter Bud Nangle said, "There were several airplanes circling to watch as the caravan continued on to Rockford. Women with babies in their arms; teenagers with searching eyes that sought out the 10 players among the tremendous caravan; sign-bearing youngsters saluting the champions, and people from all northern Illinois communities roared a warm greeting."

David Condon, the Chicago Tribune "Wake of The News" columnist who later was inducted into the Illinois Basketball Hall of Fame for his sportswriting, said the 10-car caravan that left Champaign "grew until it stretched 11 miles. One Rockford newspaper reporter, traveling out to join the motorcade, cut into line as the 196th car, and there was a seemingly endless string behind him."

Gleason reported that, "The team still was more than eight miles from Rockford when 'foot troops' joined the celebration. These were hardy souls who had abandoned their cars to stand in the rain and cheer their heroes as the motor procession reached New Milford, a Rockford suburb. It took 13 minutes to travel a mile. The street was jammed with parked cars."

Nangle said, "The biggest melee started where route 51 splits into four lanes. Three police cars spread to occupy three lanes and spearhead the parade that had grown to an estimated 500 vehicles. Upon hitting the city limits, cars were three abreast all the way back on the four lane route 51."

Warrior fans crowded highways for miles leading back into Rockford from Champaign, and city streets were even more jammed. Jubilant fans decked out their cars with red and black West High streamers and welcoming signs hailing their conquering heroes. Despite rain and chilly temperatures, thousands abandoned their cars and mobbed the happy Warriors coming home with the championship trophy.

On 11th Street, just inside the city limits, Police Captain Paul Pirello and Winnebago County Sheriff Leonard Friberg organized the official parade through the city. Fans and photographers mobbed the players and coaches as they were transferred into convertibles. Police department motorcycles, a police ambulance, and two of the city's huge fire department rigs led the parade with lights flashing and sirens wailing. A calliope and Dixieland band on a flatbed trailer followed. The championship trophy rode atop Fire Chief Wayne Swanson's car. West's cheerleaders were in a car preceding one carrying Coach Saudargas followed by four cars carrying the championship team. Trailing behind were thousands of cars, described by police as the largest entourage in the city's history.

The Tribune's Condon said Captain Pirello estimated there were about 30,000 cars on the streets, most of them decked out in rain-soaked red and black crepe paper, and 75,000 to 100,000 men, women, and children. "Traffic slowed the caravan to a pace that required more than two hours to progress from the city limits to West High school," a distance of 11 miles. The parade moved up 11th Street to Charles Street, then to State Street, and finally onto Rockton Avenue. All along the parade route prolonged horn blasts from thousands of cars amplified the din created by screaming sirens, clanging firetruck bells, blaring Dixieland music, and cheering Warrior fans.

Captain Pirello told Gleason, "He had not seen anything like it since Rockford celebrated the end of World War II in 1945. Warrior fans were leaning from apartment building windows and thousands risked pneumonia by standing in the rain, No city held a state championship reception under more adverse conditions. When the convoy crossed the Rock River into West Rockford's home territory, the tops came down on the 10 convertibles that carried the team. The regulars were soaked and so were the reserve players, but nobody cares when you have just won the Sweet 16 championship."

Wrapped in newspapers to stay warm and dry, two young Warrior fans wait for hours to see their triumphant Warriors' homecoming.

When the parade reached the intersection of Rockton Avenue and Auburn Street, just five blocks south of West High, the crowd was so great it took another 15 minutes to reach the school where the victory celebration was planned.

"The flags and bunting and ribbons along the parade route were soggy with rain, but a cloudburst could not put out the fire of enthusiasm," a Rockford newspaper editorial reported. "Throughout the afternoon, thousands of cars went by, taking every parking place on the parade route, backing up into the side streets. People gathered along the sidewalks. A drizzle came up, and then the rain, but not a car pulled away. Umbrellas and blankets covered bystanders.

"Then came the confused wailing of a score of sirens, the clangor of firetruck bells, and the piece de resistance of the parade appeared — the team itself. West High youngsters who had preceded the caravan to the school grounds broke into a dead run to surround the open cars in which the West team and coach Alex Saudargas were riding and practically carry them to the school. They were the boys and girls to whom the team belonged most especially, although it belonged to the entire city from the moment that last miraculous basket was tossed in from the playing floor Saturday night."

Coach Saudargas and the team finally arrived at West High for a brief celebration. "The players, tired, awed, and soggy were crowded around a microphone to hear official welcomes and congratulations," Johnston said. "Then they escaped to their dressing room to dry out and enjoy one of the few moments of relative privacy they've had since nailing down the championship Saturday night."

But the whirlwind day was not over for Coach Saudargas and Alice. "I got out of the car and stood in the rain when we arrived at West," she said, "but I didn't go inside. The Olsons brought me home because I was really beat and was having severe pains. When Alex arrived home, he told me he had to go to one of the television stations at 10 p.m. By then I was really in labor, so he took me to the hospital."

Through the night and into the next day of Warrior celebration, Coach Saudargas again carried an extra but hidden weight of worry.

A double welcoming

"No matter what happens at the formal welcome home for the new Illinois champion in the gym at West High School 10 o'clock Monday morning, Rockford still will be rocking from the effects of the impromptu soirée Sunday."
— Bill Gleason, Chicago American

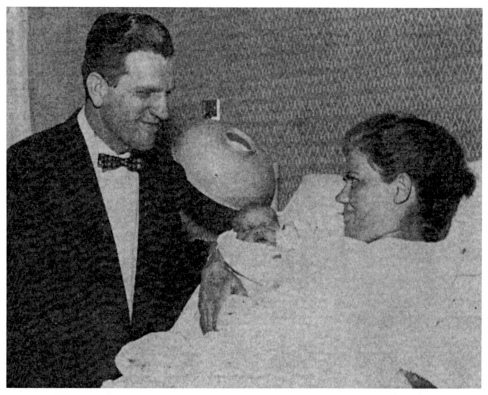

While Rockford was celebrating West High's 1955 state basketball championship, Coach Saudargas and Alice were sharing a concealed concern about their newborn daughter's medical condition. Patty was born only about 12 hours after the Warrior caravan arrived back in Rockford from the tournament in Champaign. Born premature and jaundiced, she received transfusions and remained in the hospital for a month before she was able to join her family at home.

It's Only a Game

On Monday morning, Rockford's euphoric exuberance was concentrated in the West High gym.

"Students at both West and East High Schools had to report for classes as usual Monday," Rockford sportswriter Jim Johnston said, "but the similarity between this and any other school day ended right there, Classes were dismissed almost immediately. By 10 a.m., East students had joined their West brethren for a giant pep rally in the West gymnasium. For most it was as noisy a celebration as Sunday's."

But citywide jubilation seemed remote for Coach Saudargas and Alice at Rockford Memorial Hospital where Monday morning brought them heartache. "I was in labor through the night," Alice said, "and our baby was born a little after 6 a.m. She was jaundiced and premature. She was so bright in color she looked like an orange pumpkin, just as orange/ yellow as could be. When the doctor came in, he told me she was in bad shape and was not expected to live. He said, 'If you would like to have her baptized, do it now.' I called our pastor, and they pulled in a couple nurses so they could witness it and write their names on the baptismal certificate. She was baptized somewhere between seven and eight o'clock."

Less than two hours later, Coach Saudargas had to leave the hospital and travel five blocks south for the Warriors' victory celebration at the school. Chicago Tribune writer David Condon noted that "Alex Saudargas, the coach who Saturday directed Rockford West High School to the state basketball crown, was one of the few homefolk with his mind centered on other matters today as this Winnebago County metropolis wound up its championship celebration," but Coach Saudargas concealed his concern from the exuberant packed house.

Stirring anthems by the West High band dressed in full uniform for the rally roused the standing-room-only assembly to a fever pitch. As the school song reverberated from the rafters, spirited cheerleaders from both East and West High led the throng's outbursts of wild enthusiasm for Rockford's new state champions.

Principal Blue quieted the assembly and introduced WROK president John Dixon as master of ceremonies. Dixon coordinated presentations by a bevy of assembly speakers, including Mayor Lundstrom, school board President Elmer Jepson, local media personalities, representatives of East and West High School student bodies, parent leaders of school academic and sports committees, and representatives of Rockford's earlier championship teams.

Dixon and Blue relayed congratulatory messages for the Warriors from Governor William Stratton, Illinois Senator Everett Dirksen, the Rockford Chamber of Commerce, coaches and administrators at other schools, and from other organizations and individuals throughout the state.

Then Coach Saudargas, calm and focused, strode to the microphone to introduce his champion Warriors. He started by announcing the birth of his daughter as if nothing were amiss. Condon reported that, "A weary Alex said he was pondering a name for the seven pound, three-and-a-half ounce Saudargas daughter who checked into this world only 14 hours after Alice had returned home from the tournament in Champaign," and said thunderous applause greeted Coach Saudargas' birth announcement and his introduction of the Warriors.

Rod Coffman, a favorite of both East and West High students, recalled the scene: "On one side of the floor were all the West High students and on the other side of the floor were all the East High students. As players were being introduced, everyone was being given a big hand. I had been an east-sider and had played at East as a sophomore, so East High students felt I was their contribution to the championship. When I was introduced, both sides of the floor, the whole place went crazy."

Condon said Coach Saudargas "drew another big hand in forecasting that the state title might be difficult to wrest away from West next season." To some, that may have sounded like a mere crowd-pleasing bromide, but the man who said it meant it — and his forecast would prove to be prophetic.

At the end of the assembly, school was dismissed for the day, but the celebrating continued unabated. Monday night Rockford City Council passed a resolution honoring the Warriors. On Tuesday the Illinois house and senate in Springfield passed resolutions of congratulations praising the Warriors as the "finest team in the state." Thursday Rockford Rotary honored the Warriors with a noon luncheon, cutting into school time. That evening the Junior Chamber of

Rockford Rotary honored West High's Warriors and cheerleaders at a luncheon featuring a championship trophy display. Left to right are Warrior cheerleaders Sue Swanson and Julie Applequist, Rotary President Joseph Bean, WROK sportscaster Morey Owens, Rotarian Kurt Scharbau, Pat Terranova, and Jan Stenholm.

Commerce held a banquet in honor of Coach Saudargas and the Warriors. Friday night the Warriors were honored guests at a dance arranged by the sophomore class. Two days later the Warriors were guests at afternoon and evening band concerts. They also appeared on a special WREX-TV program and were guests on Dolph Stanley's program in Beloit, WI. The days that followed included a noon Lions Club banquet, a West End Businessmen's Association evening banquet, an Elks Club evening banquet, a noon Kiwanis Club banquet, an East High Athletic Association lettermen's banquet, and more. Later the Chicago Press Club honored the Warriors along with former and current Chicago Cubs, including Manager Stan Hack.

Both principal Blue and Coach Saudargas were concerned about the impact of the heavy celebrity tour schedule on the Warriors' academics. Coach Saudargas' entire team held higher grade averages than any other cross section of the student body, and Gentry was president of the National Honor Society chapter at West High. When Principal Blue decided to terminate activities that cut into school time, Coach Saudargas agreed.

"My husband was very big on academics," Alice said. "He would tell the kids, 'You know, you're not going to be playing basketball all your life. You need an education so you can go out and find work and support yourself. This is fun now for you in high school, and you should enjoy it, but you have to do a good job in school so you can go on to college or do whatever you want to do with your education.'"

To drive home that point for his players, Coach Saudargas invited Jesse Owens, four-time Olympic gold medalist in sprints and the long jump, to be principal speaker at West High's Annual Sports Banquet weeks later. The African American athlete was renowned both for setting National Collegiate Athletic Association records at Ohio State University, where he was known as "the Buckeye Bullet," and for his 1936 Berlin Olympic victories that derailed attempts by Adolph Hitler and his National Socialist Workers Party to use the Olympics as a showcase for their Aryan supremacy doctrine.

Olympic Gold Medal Winner Jesse Owens

"Owens really laid it on the line for us," Coach Don Krieschbaum said. A Rockford newspaper account with the headline "Owens cites responsibilities" summarized his message. "Jesse Owens, one of the greatest champions of them all, hurled a challenge at 163 West High letter winners, including the 1955 Illinois state basketball champions.

"'Championships can be fleeting things,' Owens said. 'Banners gather dust, signs rust, and trophies corrode. The champions of today must avoid the pitfall of being an athletic bum of tomorrow.

"'The one purpose of an institution of learning,' reminded Owens, 'is to get an education. Athletes must learn from their coaches a code of ethics which must carry over into later life. If you carry this code of ethics into your home and your community,' he said, 'you can win the greatest championship of them all — the one which never gathers dust.' He cited four avenues of responsibility for the young athletes: the home, the community, the school, and the church."

Jesse Owens, left, talks sports and education with Coach Saudargas, Rod Coffman, standing, and Rex Parker.

Meanwhile Coach Saudargas and Alice received good news on the home front. Their daughter had defied the original prognosis. "She received three blood transfusions and was in the hospital for a month," Alice said, "but she survived, and my blood pressure, which had been off the charts, returned to normal."

Naming the Saudargas baby turned out to be another Warrior team project. On Saturday in Champaign, Alice had agreed to the players' request that the baby be named by drawing a winner from a hat with players' first names on slips of paper. When the cheerleaders found out about the arrangement, they asked that their names be placed in the hat if the baby turned out of be a girl. The winner was Patty Terranova, a junior who had been honored as one of the five outstanding cheerleaders at the state tournament by the Champaign News-Gazette. In honor of the victorious Warriors, Alice and Alex added the middle name Victoria. Patty Victoria continued progressing during the months ahead.

Alice received a basketball honor herself the Wednesday after the championship; the Chicago Tribune named her "coach of the year" in a sports page editorial: "For Illinois coach of the year, this department nominates Mrs. Alice Saudargas of Rockford. Mrs. Saudargas, we feel safe in assuming, coaches her husband, Alex, who coached the state high school basketball champions from Rockford West High School. Fourteen hours after returning from Champaign, where she shared her husband's travail as his team battled its way to the championship, she gave birth to her tenth child and fifth daughter. That was cutting it almost as close as the team's two point margin for the championship, scored in the last half minute of play, but again the timing was adequate if not comfortable."

As life returned to normal at home and at school, Coach Saudargas looked to the future for his players. "I know that he spent many afternoons making long distance phone calls to different colleges and universities to see what scholarships they could offer West athletes," Alice said. "It didn't make any difference if it was one of his basketball players, a tennis player, a football player, a baseball player, or a swimmer. He was trying to help all of them."

Coach Saudargas was also looking to the future for rebuilding his Warrior team that had been decimated by graduations. But before his rebuilt Warriors could take the floor for their first game of the new season, his rebuilding effort was disrupted by drama in the school auditorium.

A rocky start

"Some of the vows made last March by Rockford West are coming back to haunt the Warriors this year. In the midst of the tumult that surrounded West's state cage triumph at Champaign last spring, there were dominant vows of, 'We shall return.' But a lot of things can happen in nine months, and Coach Alex Saudargas and his players have found that out."

— *Bud Nangle, Chicago Daily News*

New talent stepped forward in 1956 to take up the state championship mantle Coach Saudargas and his Warriors won the previous year. Sixty percent of the West High team that went to Champaign in 1955 was lost to graduation, but Coach Saudargas molded their successors into Illinois' top basketball squad. The 1956 state champion Warriors are, front row, left to right: Tom Blake, Nolden Gentry, Johnny Wessels, Don Slaughter, Robert "Bobby" Washington, and Coach Saudargas. Second row: George Cotone, Sam Patton, Dan Seidelmann, Craig Peeples, Jack Flynn, Roscoe Burke, and Manager Bruce Wolff. Back row: Tom Urnezis, Robert Olson, Jay Heath, Roger Peacock, Conway Johnson, and Chad Coffman.

"Everybody's Asking the Same Question."

As autumn leaves fell and football gear was stowed away for another year, high school basketball and West High's Warriors became the talk of the town — and of the entire state.

"Everywhere I go," Rockford sportswriter Jim Johnston said, "somebody is popping the question: 'Will the Warriors win the state championship again?'"

Coach Saudargas parried the question with references to the tournament's 47-year history. "Well, the record books are against us," he told a reporter for the Monday Morning Mail, "but it has been done before by two teams, Elgin and Mt. Vernon."

He parried the question because graduation left him with four gaping holes to fill in his lineup. Gone were his forward Fred Boshela, a tough rebounder and high scorer when the chips were down. Gone were his playmaking guards Rex Parker and Rod Coffman, who also could be counted on to come through in the clutch with surefire outside shooting. Gone was sixth man Don Grabow, who was cited as the best sixth man in the tournament by sportswriters covering the action.

When practice opened for the new season, seventy Warrior hopefuls showed up to try out for the team. Coach Saudargas reviewed the new prospects, then cut the roster to 18 players, holding open a half dozen varsity slots for players expected to report when football ended.

At the core of his roster were senior veterans from the championship season, Nolden Gentry and Johnny Wessels. Both now topped out at 6'7" after growing an inch during the summer and both had added brawn and bulk; Gentry weighed in at 180 and Wessels 190. Rockford sportswriter Byron Baxter described them as "the kind of fun-loving players who can scare the shorts off of opposition before the game starts — palming a basketball in each hand, waving it around, and ramming dunk shots down through the hoop like cannon balls."

Junior reserves from the championship roster returning for their senior year and aiming to replace Parker and Coffman at guards were 5'9" Bobby Washington and 5'11" Sam Patton; aiming to replace Boshela at forward were 6'3" Don Slaughter and 6'2" Joe DiGiovanni. Other seniors making the preseason A-list as possible starters at the guard positions were 5'10" LaVerne Sherer, 6'1 Tom Blake, 6'2" Craig Peeples, and 5'9" Roscoe Burke. They were joined by 5'10" junior Jack Flynn.

Washington, the smallest Warrior, quickly established himself at guard with behind the back dribbling and 30 foot jump shots. He told school newspaper reporter Dick Parrott, "I can't go over them like Gentry, but I can go around and under them."

Slaughter was a late bloomer but was proving to be an able replacement for Boshela. "When we came to West High from Washington Junior High," Gentry said, "Don was about 6'1" and probably weighed 75 pounds. He wasn't even good enough to play on the sophomore team, but he went to the Montague House every night and practiced and practiced. By the time he was a senior, he was a fine basketball player." Coach Saudargas told Baxter, "Slaughter's more versatile than Boshela was, a better outshooter, better on the fast break, and real good on defense."

But before Coach Saudargas could begin piecing together and testing a new team, he was blindsided by the loss of a key player. Disciplinary action sidelined his star center Johnny Wessels when he was suspended from school.

Wessels got into trouble at a West High stage production he attended with Rod Coffman and another friend. Coffman was not eligible for basketball, but had returned to West in the fall to make up for the semester he missed when he dropped out of East High. All three had dates with girls in the show, Coffman said, "and we decided to buy a bottle of whiskey for the cast party. We didn't even like whiskey, but you could mix it with Coke so you could stomach it. I was the oldest, so I went to the liquor store to buy it." At age 18, he was three years under the legal age to purchase liquor in Illinois, but the clerk sold it to him when Coffman proffered his barely legible draft card as an ID.

"I had my topcoat on because we were dressed for the theater," Coffman said. "It was just a small bottle, so I stuck it in my coat pocket, a pretty deep pocket. We had seats right in the middle of the audience, right in the middle of a row. When we stood up to go out at intermission, I picked up my topcoat and the bottle slid out of my pocket onto the concrete floor. It burst open and the whiskey ran down toward the stage.

"We pretended like, 'What was that?' and 'Where did that come from?' and worked our way out. We did not go back in, which was a mistake because the broken glass was under our seats and everyone knew us. We were scared to death and hoped it would just blow over and that no one would make a big deal of it.

"When we got to school Monday morning, I wasn't in class ten minutes before the phone rang and I was summoned to the principal's office. Two sheriff's deputies were waiting for me with John and my other friend who was with us Saturday night. We confessed and were suspended from school. They took me to the sheriff's office because I was the one who bought the whiskey.

"The next morning we were headline news in the Rockford paper and there was a big front page article about it. That's how important high school basketball was. My brothers were angry with me and my dad was upset.

"Sheriff Kirk King, a big, rotund guy, was very nice about it. He got me into his office and said, 'You know, Rod, I did a lot worse when I went to high school, but my hands are tied here because you and Wessels are so well known.' He told me when he was in high school, he would attend the fall semester to play football, then drop out and work till school started the next fall so he could play football again. He did that for six years. Rules didn't prohibit it in those days. 'There's no way what you did should be such a big deal,' he said. 'If it were anybody else, nobody would care.'

"Then the FBI started hassling me because they found out I used my draft card as the ID. They thought I had changed the date on it, a federal offense. I showed them the draft card. It was all beat up because it was in my billfold, but I hadn't changed the date and it showed I was age 18.

"We went through bad times after that. We were outcasts. Nobody wanted to be around us. It was awful. Poor John, it lasted the whole season for him. It was in the Chicago papers, and no matter where he played, they would yell, 'Hey, you want a bottle?' He took the brunt of it." Coach Don Kriechbaum said, "I felt, and I think the team did, too, that those guys had jeopardized our championship hopes. It was a heck of a risk to take."

Coach Saudargas tried to make the best of the situation, but Chicago Daily News sportswriter Bud Nangle said, "Wessels' absence has hindered the Warriors in that Saudargas hasn't been able to work together a unit that figures to carry the burden most of the year."

Coach Saudargas experimented with lineups in the opening game against the Davenport, IA, Blue Devils. He moved Gentry to center in place of Wessels. He tried Joe DiGiovanni, Tom Blake, and Don Slaughter at the forwards and teamed Bobby Washington with Sam Patton and Craig Peeples at the guards. His makeshift Warriors prevailed over Davenport 78-62 for their 19th straight win, and Coach Saudargas was able to observe his entire roster when he emptied his bench in the third quarter.

"Gentry showed signs of unfamiliarity with the pivot post he played most of the time," Johnston said, "but he still set the pace with 26 points and turned in some flashy defensive work. He was at his best on a couple of occasions when Coach Saudargas moved 6'2" Joe DiGiovanni into the pivot and let Gentry roam his familiar forward position. Most of the remaining scoring was by Don Slaughter, with 16 points; Bobby Washington, with 13; and Tom Blake with 12."

Warrior pride took a hit the next night when Moline's Maroons ended the Warriors' 19-game winning streak, 62-55. "They were tough," Washington said. "They beat us by seven points, but that was the only game we lost, and the only reason we lost was that we didn't have John. We put Nolden at center, moved Tom Blake down to forward and brought in Flynn to play guard." Gentry led the Warriors' scoring again with 18 points, followed by Slaughter with 11. Coach Saudargas used only six players in the game. Jack Flynn replaced Sam Patton at guard and chipped in 10 points. Washington and Blake added eight each.

Warrior pride took another hit when the first Associated Press and United Press International polls for the new season were released. Both polls gave Pinkneyville's Panthers the number one spot as the team most favored to win the state championship. The Warriors were rated number two. "That's fine with me," Coach Saudargas told a school newspaper reporter. "It'll give our boys something to shoot for."

And shoot for it they did, starting with the opening tipoff against their next nonconference opponent, Belvidere. Coach Saudargas started DiGiovanni at center, moved Gentry back to his original forward position with Slaughter, and teamed Blake with Washington at guard. Within minutes of the tipoff, the Warriors ran up a 10-0 lead and never looked back. By halftime the lead had grown to 45-21. The final tally was 82-62. Gentry again led the scoring with 30 points, followed by Slaughter with 24. DiGiovanni added nine, Washington eight, Blake five, Flynn four, and Patton two.

Wessels' suspension had ended, but he didn't suit up for the Belvidere game. "He's practicing," Coach Saudargas told Rockford sportswriter Byron Baxter, "but he has to make up some studies before he can play. He'll be back eventually. His return is another reason for getting the boys back to their original positions. When he comes back, all he has to do is take over at center."

Wessels returned with a vengeance against Rochelle, the last nonconference warm-up game for the Warriors. He led the team to an 83-42 romp, pouring in 22 points, 18 of them in the first half. Gentry added 15 and Slaughter 12. Washington exploded for nine of his 11 points in the second quarter, giving the Warriors a 43-16 halftime lead. Flynn added six free throws and four from the floor in the fourth quarter.

With four wins and one loss in nonconference competition, Coach Saudargas had his starting five in place, backed up by top reserves Flynn and DiGiovanni. Big Eight Conference play started the following week against two conference powerhouses, the Elgin Maroons, 5-1 in nonconference games, followed by the undefeated LaSalle-Peru Cavaliers.

Barrel-clad Winnebago County Sheriff Kirk King, reminiscent of Jefferson Davis "J.D." Hogg in the TV sitcom Dukes of Hazzard, was Rockford's "Boss Hogg". King's antics in high school and as sheriff made him sympathetic with Rod Coffman when he and Johnny Wessels got into trouble prior to the 1956 season opener.

"Déjà vu all over again"

"West opens its Big Eight Conference season hosting Elgin. Thus the 1955-56 campaign will begin just as it ended. Does Coach Saudargas think West can repeat as state champions? 'I don't want to hang myself out on any limb,' he said, 'but let's be honest. This is a good team. Our front line is probably better than it was last year; our guards are sharp, not as tough and good defensively, perhaps, but they're better scorers. Do I think we can win again? Yes, I'd say the chances are good.'"

— Jerry Holtzman, Chicago Sun-Times

Warriors Forever

Going for "The Big Prize"

"As I see it," Rockford sportswriter Jim Johnston said in a preseason assessment, "there are five major factors which determine whether a team can go all the way for the big prize — coaching, talent, experience, caliber of opposition, and that intangible something which you can chalk up as spirit, poise, desire, or something else.

"With the Warriors, coaching is a constant factor. Coach Alex Saudargas certainly has proven his great ability. Talent and experience, in this case, go together, and there seems to be no shortage of either at West. Before the Warriors can even consider a bid to defend their state title, they must worry about defending the Big Eight crown, and the caliber of opposition will be greatly improved over last year.

"So that leaves the inexplainable 'something' as the key to Warrior success. Are they hungry enough now? Will they jell again as an unbeatable unit? Will they have that poise and spirit? Time alone will tell, and upon that rests their chances."

First up to test the Warriors' mettle in Big Eight Conference play was Elgin, the team that came in second in the conference and second in the '55 state tournament. Any doubts Johnston had about the Warriors were eased from the tipoff. "The Warriors never trailed," he wrote afterwards. "Slaughter put the show on the road with five quick points. Blake made it 7-0 by stealing the ball and driving in for a layup. West expanded a 14-8 first quarter lead to 35-24 by halftime. The second half was just more of the same before the Warriors finally made it a 77-56 rout.

"Wessels scored half of West's 14 points in the first quarter, but had to take a rest when he picked up his fourth foul only three minutes into the second. He tossed in eight more in the third before fouling out in the opening seconds of the final period." Washington led the scoring with 16 points. Wessels and Gentry each chipped in 15, and Slaughter 14. Blake scored five and DiGiovanni added three when he filled in for Wessels.

Only one game remained before the holiday break from school, a road game against the LaSalle-Peru Cavaliers. They were undefeated in preseason play and were tough to beat on their home court, but the Warriors rolled over them 58-43, hitting at a .511 clip. Wessels scored 24 points despite getting into foul trouble again with four fouls in the first half. He avoided fouling out and scored 14 of his points in the last two quarters. Gentry scored 11 and controlled the boards with help from Slaughter. Blake added eight points, Slaughter seven, Washington six, and Flynn two.

From that point on until Super-Sectional tournament action in March, the Warriors steamrollered opponents with a margin of victory averaging 27 points. No one came closer than 12.

During the annual East High-West High round robin Christmas tournament, the Warriors defeated Peoria-Manual 72-47 and Peoria-Central 67-52. When they coasted by conference foe East Aurora 75-53 in the first action of the New Year, both Associated Press and United Press International named the Warriors the number one team in the state. Pinkneyville dropped to second. The Warriors remained in the top spot for the rest of the year.

After East Aurora, the Warriors avenged their only 1955 loss by defeating Rock Island 79-67 and then easily disposed of Freeport 73-50. Waiting in Rockford to challenge the rampaging Warriors next was their archrival across the Rock River, the East High E-Rabs. The game matched the Big Eight's highest scoring offense against the league's best defense. East had scored 286 points in conference play and runner-up West 283.

But West had allowed only 202 points and East was seventh in the league on defense, allowing 281.

Rockford sportswriter Ray Lloyd's pregame description of the East-West battle as "one of Illinois' fiercest high school basketball rivalries" seemed like an understatement in the wake of the fracas that followed. Referees called 68 personal fouls and two technical fouls in the course of the melee; five players fouled out and five more East High players had four personal fouls.

East jumped off to a 5-0 lead in the first minutes of play when guard Gary Lindsay hit four free throws and forward Fred Clow added one while Wessels missed three, Gentry two, and Slaughter one. Then Wessels and Slaughter combined for nine straight points to give the Warriors a lead they held and increased the rest of the way.

"Pent-up emotions, tempers, and frequent blasts of whistles kept the overflow throng of fans at East High in a dither of frenzy," Johnston reported, and it was an indicator of things to come when Lindsay fouled out with a minute and 18 seconds left in the first quarter.

West edged ahead 15-11 at the end of the quarter and led 34-26 at the half, but "it was the third quarter," Lloyd wrote, "which sent the partisan East crowd of 3,000 into roars of disapproval with the fouling out of E-Rab favorite Fred Clow and assessment of technical fouls against Clow and another East hero, Joe Choppi. During the spree, Wessels hit seven of eight free throws, Slaughter hit five of seven, Gentry three of four, and Washington two of two. West closed the period with a rush of 12 straight points which sent the score to 59-34 and left East completely out of it." In the midst of the ruckus, a fan stormed onto to the floor to argue with a referee and had to be restrained by an E-Rab.

Gentry and Washington fouled out in the fourth quarter and East outscored West 27-21, but it was not enough to overcome the Warrior lead, and West emerged on top 80-61. Warrior poise on the free throw line made the difference. East outscored West by 12 from the floor, but West overcame the deficit by sinking 46 of 67 free throws, hitting on 69 percent of their shots, while East made only 15 of 37, a 41 percent accuracy rate.

Wessels finished with 29 points, Slaughter 15, Washington 13, Blake eight, and Gentry seven.

With the Wessels scoring machine pouring in points, West steamrolled opponents in the next seven games, outscoring them by 186 points, 568 to 382, with no victory margin narrower than 13 points.

West Aurora fell 91-49 with Wessels dropping in 29 points, Gentry 20, Slaughter 18, Washington 12, and Blake five.

Four Warriors scored double digits in a 79-41 rout of DeKalb. Slaughter lead the scoring with 18 points. Wessels played only about half the game and added 15, Gentry and Flynn 14 each, and Blake nine.

The Warriors sewed up at least a share of the Big Eight Conference title in their next game when they downed LaSalle-Peru 74-49. Wessels had his third 29 point night, including 13 of 17 free throws. Slaughter added 17, Gentry 12, Blake 10, and Washington six.

The following night Wessels topped his previous scoring highs with 32 points in the Warrior 83-62 defeat of nonconference opponent Sterling. Gentry added 18, Slaughter 16, and Washington two.

With a 71-58 victory over Joliet, the Warriors clinched their fourth undisputed Big Eight conference championship in five years. Wessels again led the scoring with 22 points, followed by Slaughter with 16, Washington 15, and Gentry 13.

The following night, West entertained guests from Indiana, Horace Mann High School of Gary. Warrior hospitality ended when the nonconference game started. With double digit scoring by Wessels, Slaughter, and Gentry again leading the way, the Warriors defeated Horace Mann 82-57. Wessels tallied 24; Slaughter and Gentry 15 each; and Blake added eight.

A week later all five Warrior starters scored double digits in defeating Freeport 88-66. Wessels led the way again with 28. Slaughter added 20, Gentry 15, Washington 12, and Blake 11.

Only a home court game against their Rockford East nemesis stood between the Warriors and their second straight undefeated Big Eight championship.

"If the time for an upset of the number one ranked Warriors ever was ripe, it is now," said Rockford sportswriter Dave Pennington. "With the Westerners looking forward to tournament play next week in start of their state title defense, East is in the right spot."

Tournament fever was burning its way through West High and reached epidemic level in the Warriors' standing-room-only, packed house for the regular season wrap-up game against East High. On one end of the gym was a large map of Illinois created by Warrior students. It had a star over Rockford and showed the path from Rockford to the Super-Sectional game site in Moline and from there to the state championship game site in Champaign. Large footprints bearing starting players' names on each footstep led to the map.

Ignoring state tournament talk, Coach Saudargas told Pennington he thought the East-West matchup would be "a pretty tough game. It won't mean as much to us as it will if we meet East next Friday night in the regional finals, but we'll play the same. The kids want to win and I think East wants to show us they can do better than they did last time."

The game started out as a seesaw battle. "Blake hit two free throws to give West the lead," Johnston reported, "but Joe Choppi connected from the field to make 2-2. Washington swished one to put West ahead again. Choppi tied it at 4-4. Slaughter regained the West lead, and Fred Clow made it 6-6 before Wessels' first two free throws put West in command. East never was in front, but the E-Rabs stayed in the ball game all the way, keeping the issue in doubt until West finally pulled out of reach in the closing minutes."

Free throws again were important in the 73-61 outcome. West made 23 of 28 attempts, an 82 percent accuracy rate, while East made 19 of 28, only 47 percent. Wessels finished with 20 points before fouling out in the third quarter. Slaughter added 14, Washington and Gentry 12 each, Blake 10, and Flynn five.

The victory over East extended the Warriors' winning streak for the season to 18 and matched West's 1955 regular season record of 19 wins and one loss. It also extended the Warriors' Big Eight Conference winning streak to 21 games over three seasons. After the game, while the Warriors and their fans were whooping it up over their victory and growing even more excited about tournament prospects, Coach Saudargas received troubling news from home. His 64-year-old mother, Maxine, had died suddenly of a heart attack shortly before the start of the game.

As if to relieve their coach of a burden in the wake of his loss, the Warriors rolled through the next week's regional tournament, defeating

Hononegah 93-40, Harlem 94 to 62, and Rockford East 98-71. They delivered more of the same at the sectional tournament the following week, defeating Forreston 105-66 and overcoming Freeport's stalling efforts 49-29.

The respite for Coach Saudargas and his Warriors ended abruptly when they traveled to Moline for a Super-Sectional matchup against Galesburg. Every degree of mind, body, and spirit they possessed was about to be put to the test.

Crunch time

"We're not kidding ourselves," said Coach Saudargas. "We know how rocky the road to the state title can be. But we'll be trying."
— *Rockford sportswriter Ralph Leo*

West's Warriors were confident as they headed off to Moline for a Super-Sectional clash with Galesburg's Super Streaks. Their confidence was badly shaken within seconds of the tipoff.

In the Path of the Storm

Galesburg's Silver Streaks plowed into the Warriors like a freight train barreling down the tracks. They hit with such force that the stunned Warriors found themselves 15 points behind only minutes after the opening tipoff. The wild battle that followed was the rip-roaring start to five nerve-racking days for Coach Saudargas and his Warriors.

Ninety seconds into the game Galesburg was leading 6-4. About four minutes later, the lead had grown to 22-7. "Galesburg shut West Rockford off completely," Champaign News-Gazette sportswriter Bill Schrader said. "Many times the Warriors couldn't get the ball across the center line against the tight Galesburg full-court press."

By the end of the first quarter, the Warriors were beginning to recover from what some sportswriters called their "initial shock and bewilderment," cutting Galesburg's lead to 24-13. When Wessels and Gentry closed the gap to 26-19 with six straight points in the opening minutes of the second quarter, Galesburg switched to a stalling offense. The tactic, designed to halt the Warrior rally, slowed scoring by both teams, and the half ended 29-23.

Galesburg sharpshooter Mark Owens made it 31-23 at the beginning of the third quarter, but Wessels closed it to 31-27 with two straight baskets. At that point Coach Saudargas lost one of his starting guards when Bobby Washington was fouled and went out of the game with an eye injury. "I began seeing double," Washington said. "I went out and Jack Flynn came in for the rest of the game. He was a great, left-handed shooter, and helped us come back with his free throw scoring."

Five minutes later the Warriors had pulled to within one point, 39-38. Then Gentry was fouled and sank both free throws, giving West a 40-39 lead. By the end of the quarter, the Warriors had surged ahead 46-41. Twice in the fourth quarter the Warriors opened up seven point leads, but both times the Silver Streaks came roaring back. With 35 seconds left in the game, Galesburg edged ahead 57-56. Gentry was fouled and made one free throw to tie the game, but missed his second.

When Russ Lind grabbed the rebound for Galesburg, frenzied fans turned Wharton Fieldhouse into a madhouse, said Champaign sportswriter Bert Bertine. "Rockford's title hung in the balance as the seconds ticked off. With five seconds to go, Owens took his favorite shot. The ball dipped into the circle and out again. Gentry grabbed the rebound as regulation time ended with the big field house rocking."

West jumped off to a 61-57 lead in the three minute overtime when Wessels dropped in a layup and sank two free throws. Owens made it 61-59 with a 15-foot jump shot, but Blake followed with two free throws to put the Warriors ahead 63-59. Owens struck again with a basket and a free throw to make it 63-62. Then Flynn sank his ninth free throw in 10 attempts, but missed the bonus shot.

With the Warriors leading 64-62 and time running out, Galesburg reserve Bob Junkin fired a 12-foot jump shot that went through the net as the buzzer sounded. Tied again at 64, the Warriors and Silver Streaks were forced into a sudden-death overtime with victory going to the first team to score two points.

Galesburg got the sudden-death tipoff, but Blake stole the ball. Then Owens stole it from Wessels, but Galesburg forward Bill Granning missed a shot and Gentry came down with the rebound. "With 6,000 screaming fans swept away by the mass hysteria that accompanies a state tournament thriller," Schrader said, "Wessels tried a hook shot and missed. Gentry slapped the ball toward the basket, but it careened off the rim. The smaller Galesburg players attempted desperately to reach as high as the giant Rockford star, but it was useless. His second tip was soft. It banked off the basket and through for two points and a West Rockford victory, 66-64."

In the dressing room after the game, all Coach Saudargas could say to sportswriters was, "Oh, brother. Oh, brother. Oh, brother." And he kept saying it over and over again. "It wasn't a noisy dressing room," a reporter noted. "Gentry sat on a bench, his head between his hands, sighing and shaking his head as if he could hardly believe it all. The players seemed more relieved than happy, and most of the players were too tired to celebrate."

Bertine heard someone in the locker room comparing the Gentry tip-in win over Galesburg to the Gentry tip-in of an errant shot by Wessels for the state title win over Elgin at Huff Gym a year earlier, but "Coach Saudargas said, 'It was twice as dramatic this time. Nolden Gentry had to do it twice.' Gentry responded, 'I really felt bad when my first tip didn't go in. Then my heart gave a big jump when I saw the ball coming right back to me again.'"

Bertine said, "Gentry's worth to West was never better demonstrated than in this cliffhanger with Galesburg. It went far beyond providing the winning basket. In the first half, it was Gentry who brought the ball across the line in the face of Galesburg's press. It was Gentry who dragged down a tremendous 21 rebounds of West's 38. Galesburg got 28. It was Gentry who set up a number of West's baskets besides scoring 13 points himself.

"Coach Saudargas also called attention to an unheralded member of his cast who played a big part in the win: Jack Flynn, the only Rockford substitute. Flynn took over for Bobby Washington when Washington received an eye injury in the third quarter. The reserve relieved Gentry of most of his crossing the line duties and in the process picked up a total of 11 free throw chances, of which he sank nine. 'That was great free throwing under a lot of pressure,' Coach Saudargas said."

Wessels led Warrior scoring with 24 points. Slaughter added 16, Flynn 9, and Blake 4.

But the long night was not over for the Warriors. Waiting outside Wharton Fieldhouse was a swirling snowstorm making their long drive home even longer.

"That was about the longest night I ever hope to spend," Coach Saudargas told Bertine later. "I don't mean only the game with Galesburg. I mean afterward, too. We got home at three o'clock Wednesday morning. There was a big wreck on the road near Oregon and traffic was tied up for two hours. We went all the way back to Dixon, then got word that the road was open, so we turned right around again.

"One result was that we had hardly any practice. The boys slept through most of Wednesday, and Thursday we had the long trip down to Champaign."

As he had done the previous year, Coach Saudargas arranged for the Warriors to stop on the way to Champaign for a short workout at Illinois State University in Normal. Rex Parker, starting guard on the 1955 championship team, had a surprise waiting for them when they arrived.

The showdown

"We wanted to win so bad. I felt if you have a chance to do something, you just step up and do it."
— Bobby Washington, '56 championship clincher

WASHINGTON · FLYNN · SAUDARGAS · BLAKE
WEST 44 ROCKETS · WEST 53 XFORD · WEST 43 XFORD
PEACOCK · WESSELS · COFFMAN · GENTRY · DEEPLES · SLAUGHTER · HEATH

On Saturday morning, West High fans in Rockford pinned their hopes for a second straight championship on the Warrior squad starters and bench backups getting ready for action. Fans who were in Champaign for the tournament were encouraged by The News Gazette headline naming the Warriors the tourney favorite, but the paper prophetically cited Edwardsville as a dark horse contender capable of an upset, also.

Facing the Music

Rex Parker had enrolled at Beloit College after graduation and was playing for the freshman team there, but switched to Illinois State where his girlfriend Carol Cleveland, later his wife of more than six decades, was enrolled. Cleveland was West High's Sweet Sixteen queen and represented West at the 1955 tournament.

Parker said, "We knew that West had won the super sectional and would be stopping at Illinois State on their way to Champaign. My roommate happened to be a music major who played the French Horn. We got some of his musician friends together to play the Rockford fight song when the Warriors arrived. The kids on campus gathered around to see the Rockford team because they were predicted to win it all."

"What a surprise we got," Coach Saudargas told Schrader. "When we heard all the music, we looked out and there was Rex Parker leading about nine musicians playing the school fight song. We had a good workout. Washington isn't completely over that bump in the eye he got in the Galesburg game, but the doctors have been looking at it and say it should be completely cleared up by Friday evening."

As he checked in his defending state champion Warriors at the Inman Hotel in Champaign Thursday night, Coach Saudargas told reporters he planned no change in his starting lineup against West

Frankfort Friday despite Washington's injury. He praised Jack Flynn for helping defeat Galesburg with nine free throws and with his dribbling and ball-handling ability that foiled Galesburg's full-court press, but said, "Why change now? We know Flynn's a good one, and it's nice to have a good one to put in there when you're in trouble, but Washington's okay. He'll show you tomorrow."

Rockford sportswriter Jim Johnston said there was a widely held consensus that the Warriors' starting five was destined to win it all. "At least a dozen veteran coaches and sportswriters figure the state championship was decided Tuesday night at Moline's Wharton Fieldhouse," Johnston said. Friday's quarterfinal game against West Frankfort and Saturday's semifinal against Dunbar of Chicago seemed to confirm their consensus.

"West Rockford's Warriors waltzed to an easy 82-70 triumph over West Frankfort," Johnston wrote after the Warrior's quarterfinal victory Friday. Never behind in the game, the Warriors scored at a blistering .531 rate, with Wessels pouring in 36 points. Slaughter added 14, Blake 10, Gentry nine, and Washington eight.

It was more of the same in Saturday afternoon's semifinal match against Dunbar of Chicago. "West Rockford was superior under the boards and Dunbar was suffering a miserable shooting afternoon," said Chicago American sportswriter Tommy Kouzmanoff. "The Warriors snuffed out the Chicago area's last hope for the state title, crushing Dunbar by a surprising 61-48 score." Don Slaughter led the Warrior offense, pouring in 11 points during a third quarter surge that gave the Warriors a 17 point lead.

"Don Slaughter, that was the kid who killed us," Dunbar Assistant Coach Tony Mafia told Champaign sportswriter Ira Lurvey. "We had their big boy, John Wessels, stopped up pretty much earlier in the game, but we never figured on Slaughter."

Lurvey said Coach Saudargas heaped praise on Slaughter, too: "He's a great ballplayer. It's just that with Gentry and Wessels always around, he seldom gets the publicity he deserves."

Coach Dutch Rittmeyer cited Gentry's play: "You can't discount that defensive performance turned in by Nolden Gentry. He stopped our high scorer, Mel Davis, and that gummed up everything for us."

Slaughter led Warrior scoring with 19 points despite fouling out halfway through the fourth quarter. Wessels added 18, Gentry 11, Washington nine, Blake three, and Flynn one.

All that stood between the Warriors and their second straight championship was the tournament's grand finale Saturday night. In that battle, the Warriors faced the high-scoring sharpshooters of the Edwardsville Tigers. Sportswriters billed the contest as:

— North versus South: Rockford, at the top of Illinois, 15 minutes from the Wisconsin border, versus Edwardsville, 275 miles to the south, 30 minutes from St. Louis;

— Height versus shooting: the Warriors' front line stood 6'7", 6'7", and 6'3 versus Edwardsville's 6'3 1/2", 6'2 1/2" and 6' 1 1/2", but Edwardsville's marksmen hit at a consistent .550 rate versus the Warriors' average of about .450;

West High cheerleaders welcomed a new member who joined their squad for the championship battle with Edwardsville. Pat Flannery was a state tournament icon, attending and cheering for any team from northern Illinois every year since 1913. Flannery is flanked here, left to right, by Mary Canfield, Jean Davis, Patty Terranova, and Jan Stenholm.

— A matchup pitting against each other the four players considered the best in Illinois: the Tigers' Mannie Jackson and Govonor Vaughn versus the Warriors' Nolden Gentry and Johnny Wessels.

Huff Gymnasium was packed to its 7,000 standing room only capacity for the clash while fans from border to border in Illinois and in neighboring areas of five adjoining states tuned in on radio and TV. In Rockford, those who had to work Saturday night made arrangements to follow the game. Emergency room nurses at Rockford Memorial Hospital brought in their radios and a TV. Police and sheriff departments had radios tuned into WROK for Morey Owens' play by play description of the action. Rockford Firefighters sat down in their seven fire stations to watch the game , but worried they would be called out to fight a fire.

The only fire they had to worry about that night was in Champaign where hoop nets sizzled with hot shooting by both teams. Edwardsville took the opening tipoff and Govonor Vaughn immediately launched the scoring. The Tigers jumped off to 6-2 lead before the Warriors fought their way on top, 10-8. Vaughn pumped in three jump shots and Wessels responded with two baskets and four free throws as the first quarter ended with the Warriors ahead 18-14.

Vaughn and Jackson combined to score five straight points at the start of the second quarter, putting the Tigers in front 19-18. The Warriors answered with nine straight points for the biggest lead of the game, 27-19. Following another exchange of baskets, Edwardsville poured in ten straight points to retake the lead, 31-29.   Wessels added two free throws and Jackson one before Slaughter hit on a jump shot to end the half with the Warriors on top 33-32. Vaughn and Jackson scored all but two of the Tigers' second quarter points, and Wessels scored all but three for the Warriors.

Everyone got into the scoring act in the third period, and the Warriors appeared to be pulling away, leading 54-48 at quarter's end. Only seconds into the fourth frame Edwardsville closed the gap to 54-51. Then Washington hit with a jump shot and Gentry sank two free throws to make it 58-51.

With a little over five minutes remaining on the clock, Vaughn and Jackson combined for three baskets in 56 seconds, closing the gap to 58-57 and setting off pandemonium in Huff Gym. Two minutes later, with the Warriors leading 60-59, Coach Saudargas called for a stalling offense.

With 1:10 left, Wessels connected and the game entered a gut-wrenching final minute with the Warriors on top 62-59. Vaughn hit 10 seconds later, narrowing the score to 62-61. With 33 seconds remaining, Gentry sank two free throws to make it 64-61. Five seconds later Vaughn hit again, closing the gap to 64-63.

Washington was fouled deliberately a few seconds later. With the capacity crowd on its feet and Huff Gym exploding in a deafening roar, Washington sank two free throws to put the Warriors ahead by three once again, 66-63. The Tigers raced down the court and, with eight seconds remaining, Ken Shaw scored to make it a one point game, 66-65. Amid the uproar and hysteria gripping Warriors' and Tigers' backers as the clock ticked off the final seconds, Washington was fouled deliberately again. He walked to the free throw line and sank the game-clincher for the Warriors. He missed his second shot, but with only two seconds left on the clock it was too late for Edwardsville to score. The scoreboard read 67-65, and the Warriors were the Illinois state basketball champions for the second year in a row — and again by a two point margin in a down-to-the-last-seconds nail-biter.

Police and security were unable to restrain frenzied fans. It took them about 30 minutes to restore order so trophies could be presented, but it was another hour of interviews and photos before exhausted Warriors were able to straggle into the dressing room. Schrader said Bobby Washington was the first to arrive. "'Boy, oh boy, oh boy,' sighed Washington as he sank to a bench. 'How does it feel to be a hero?' he was asked. 'No, no, no,' insisted Bobby, whose 17 points topped any of his previous efforts in scoring. 'We all did it.'"

When Coach Saudargas arrived mopping his brow another hour later, he told sportswriters: "Bobby Washington carried us to our second state championship. He got the clutch baskets when we needed them. He got the clutch free throws when we needed them. He quarterbacked the team and settled the kids down when they got jumpy. This guy has been behind the scenes all year, and he's been the 'glue' holding us together. I guess he finally decided he was going to show people what little guys are worth to a big team, and he couldn't have picked a better night. It was his best ballgame, and he was our margin of victory."

Coach Saudargas was lavish in praise for all his Warriors: Wessels, high scorer with 29 points; Gentry, who played outstanding defense and chipped in 17 points; Slaughter, who helped control the boards with his rebounding and chipped in four points; and Blake, who contributed as a playmaker and whose ball control was at the heart of the stalling offense which slowed down Edwardsville's hot shooting.

Lurvey said Coach Saudargas also praised the Tigers' Govonor Vaughn and Mannie Jackson. Vaughn poured in 13 baskets in 19 attempts and two free throws for 28 points, and Jackson 10 baskets in 21 attempts and one free throw for 21 points. "Boy, those kids from Edwardsville were shooting," Coach Saudargas told Lurvey. "Swish, swish, swish, just like that. They could drive a guy nuts. They jump and shoot from out and hit. We go out to get them and they go around us. They were two of the best shots I've ever seen."

As Coach Saudargas was speaking to reporters and the uproar was quieting down in Champaign, there was bedlam in downtown Rockford: sidewalks filled with noisy revelers, fireworks exploded off the State Street bridge, and cars with drivers leaning out the window and blowing their horns filled the streets. The Warriors were champions again!

Meanwhile some city leaders huddled in a corner of the Warrior dressing room planning for a "secret" way back to Rockford to avoid crowds along the road. Waiting to foil their plan were about 125,000 deliriously happy Warrior fans eager to greet their conquering heroes on their triumphant journey home.

"Rockford Has Most Riotous Celebration In Its History"
Associated Press Headline

"The general feeling in Rockford seemed to be summed up by one happy booster who said, 'It was rough, but we knew they could do it. We're used to winning the tough ones.'" — Associated Press

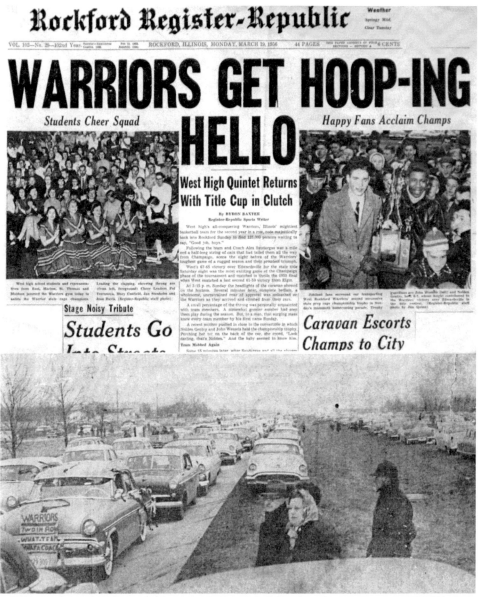

"WARRIORS TWO IN ROW. WHAT A TEAM, WHAT A COACH"
proclaims a placard on one of the thousands of cars greeting the
Warrior champions. About 125,000 to 150,000 Warrior enthusiasts
were on hand for the homecoming.

Taking the "Quiet" Road Home

"Coach Alex Saudargas sought to lead his two-time state basketball champions from Rockford West up the 'quiet' road home Sunday," Chicago Daily News sportswriter Bud Nangle said. "Instead, Saudargas, who took the Warriors up Route 47 this year after following route 51 last March, shepherded the champions into a wild, screaming, welcome home crowd that started to gang up on Saudargas and his Warriors as far away as Sycamore, 35 miles southeast of Rockford."

Rockford sportswriter Jim Johnston said the victory caravan started with six official cars and nine carloads of fans. "It lined up in front of the Inman Hotel in Champaign and started on its way at 10 a.m. It had grown to 28 cars before leaving Champaign with a police escort to the city limits. The group turned north off Route 150 at Mahomet 12 miles to the west for the long haul up Highway 47, and the caravan grew longer and longer as it moved along."

Another 100 cars joined the caravan as it turned west off Highway 47 at Route 72 and wound its way home, Nangle said, then "a mass of 300 cars greeted the caravan at the junction of Routes 51 and 72, 13 miles south of Rockford, with shrieking horns and cheers as the string of cars swung north on 51. From this point on the road was jammed with cars all the way to Rockford, with airplanes dipping in to join the celebration and a tremendous number of cars joining the procession. The line of vehicles was estimated in the thousands."

The Associated Press reported, "Sunday's outpouring ignored the 32 degree temperature and gray skies to begin forming along the parade route around noon, some three hours before the team arrived. Rockford Police Traffic Sergeant Charles Berve estimated the crowd at 125,000, but said he couldn't begin to estimate the number of cars that participated in the parade. Rockford Police Captain Paul Pirello agreed with the crowd estimate, but said it might well have been near 150,000."

Rockford sportswriter Byron Baxter described fans' frenzy when "headlights of the caravan showed on the horizon at 3:15 p.m. Several minutes later, complete bedlam, a wholehearted, unrestrained roar of approval was unleashed on the Warriors as they arrived and climbed from their cars. The surging mass knew every team member by his first name."

Nangle said players, coaches, and cheerleaders "were transferred to flashy, new convertibles for the journey through the city. The cheerleaders were in the first two convertibles, the coaches in the third, and the players in the following cars. Co-captains Nolden Gentry and John Wessels rode in the fourth car with the coveted championship trophy between them.

"Huge street sweeper's plastered with signs proclaiming 'Clean sweep by Rockford West' were in the motorcade. The traditional fire trucks carried additional gems such as 'hottest in the state' and 'Warriors set Rockford on fire.'"

Along the parade route, "stocking-capped heads of schoolboys dotted the tops of billboards like blackbirds on a telephone wire," Baxter said. "Residents of the area took their places on front porch roofs and apparently had invited their neighbors from farther down the street. A stray transient who might've been trapped in the unending line of traffic must've wondered at the magnitude of the crowd. But not for long. A look at most any one of the decked out automobiles told him West Rockford High School had won its second straight basketball championship."

Nangle said, "It took two hours to travel the 10 miles to the high school as thousands of cars, most of them double parked on both sides of the street and filled with people, were augmented by tens of thousands of wildly cheering citizens who turned out to greet the champs. At the high school, more than 5000 milled around."

About 1000 broke through a police cordon and stormed the gym for an impromptu celebration, chanting songs and cheers as the team posed for pictures. Mayor Milton Lundstrom and Principal James Blue greeted the team briefly and announced an official welcome home ceremony was scheduled for 10 a.m. Monday in the gym.

In Monday's Rockford Morning Star, Johnston started the avalanche of accolades, sharing superlatives thrown West's way by other members of the Illinois press corps covering the tournament:

"1. Greatest team ever to win the state title."

"2. Gentry and Wessels, the greatest one – two combination in tournament history."

" 3. If one college got all five Warriors, it could stop recruiting for a few years."

"4. Gentry among the greatest prep stars of all times."

At 10 a.m., the West High gym was packed for a celebration emceed by WROK sports director Morey Owens. His was the play-by-play voice that fired the imaginations of listeners all season long with vivid descriptions of Warrior action up and down the court and in the war zone under the basket. He introduced a host of speakers including Principal Blue, Mayor Lundstrom, School Board President Elmer Jepson, heads of West High education and sports committees, student representatives from West, East, Muldoon, St. Thomas, and Harlem High Schools, media guests, and others congratulating the Warriors.

Then Coach Saudargas introduced his players. Chicago Tribune sportswriter Cooper Rollow, said, "Three stars were the chief toast of the welcoming crowd — the two 6'7" stars, Johnny Wessels and Nolden Gentry, and Bob Washington. It was the 5'9" Washington who drew the greatest praise from the welcomers."

Coach Saudargas also shined the limelight on his Warriors who received fewer headlines during the season. He paraphrased a sportswriter's comment, "Slaughter is just Gentry four inches shorter." And he praised the team spirit of Tom Blake, "our big guard, a very fine ballplayer, a boy with fierce competitive spirit who sparked the team every minute; a boy who was willing to sacrifice his own scoring opportunity to feed the big boys in the front line, and who never once quit fighting."

He cited his reserves who were stars in junior varsity games and who sharpened starters' skills day in and day out at practice sessions: — 6'2" Chad Coffman, 6'6" Roger Peacock, 6'5" Jay Heath, 6'2 Craig Peeples, and 5'10" Jack Flynn who filled in so ably for the injured Washington against Galesburg.

A few hours later, Rockford Register-Republic editors echoed Coach Saudargas' words and coaching philosophy in their Monday afternoon edition: "It was truly a team victory. There were standouts in every state tournament game, but the final results were the product of team effort. When one player was bottled up or off form, another took over and came through with points when they were needed.

"To Nolden Gentry, Johnny Wessels, Don Slaughter, Bobby Washington, and Tom Blake — the first string — go the biggest cheers. But Jack Flynn showed his ability to fill in when needed, and the others on the squad — Greg Peeples, Roger Peacock, Chad Coffman, and Jay Heath – were ready had they been needed. The Warriors achieved what they set out to do — to become the third team in history to win two consecutive state championships. The odds against that feat were staggering, but West Rockford had that extra margin of superiority when it counted."

It was the storybook ending of an era, Johnston said. "One of the most fabulous two-season success stories in the annals of Illinois prep basketball was at an end today. Left in its wake by West High's magnificent Warriors were two consecutive state championships, two undefeated Big Eight Conference seasons, 58 victories, and only two defeats. A more fitting climax to this two-year cage epoch could not have been concocted by any form of witchcraft. The Warriors, every one of them, earned every superlative in the book."

Once again the Warriors were besieged by community organizations in the days and weeks following their championship. Invitations to luncheons and banquets and TV appearances and radio programs and special events poured in as they had the year before, threatening to disrupt the student-athletes' studies. But Principal Blue and Coach Saudargas were prepared for the onslaught. Luncheons and banquets were limited to one per week.

It was the end of an era, but the beginning of the Warrior legacy. Major changes lay ahead for the players, for Coach Saudargas, for Alice, for West High School, for Rockford, and for the country.

West High students chose senior cheerleader Patty Terranova and senior hoop star Nolden Gentry queen and king of the school's annual May festival in the wake of the Warriors' second consecutive state basketball championship. Terranova was on the Warrior cheerleading squad for three years and was chosen as West High's homecoming queen in the fall. Gentry's athletic honors were matched by his scholastic performance, named to the National Honor Society his junior year and society president as a senior.

Coach Saudargas, aka "Dad"

"I heard him on the phone talking to the Athletic Director at Loyola University in Chicago one afternoon. He was trying to talk him into giving a student a scholarship. After dinner, Dad and I went out and played ball, and I'm thinking, 'Here's a guy raising ten kids and a couple hundred others at the same time.' It was amazing. He was always up, always go, go, go, always happy to see you, always had something positive to say. There were times when my brothers and I screwed up, and we got severely chastised by him, but afterwards he'd sit down and talk with us. At one point, he called a little family chat among us boys when we were a little older and were starting to hang out with friends. 'Just remember one thing,' he said, 'nothing good happens after midnight.'"

— Coach Saudargas' oldest son Alex

After Coach Saudargas led his Warriors to their first state basketball championship, Rockford City Council honored Coach Saudargas as the city's Father of the Year. "There was one time when we were all sitting around the table at home," he recalled. "Some of the kids were talking about how we'd be able to afford more things if we didn't have so many children. 'That's all right, Dad,' 11-year-old Richard said, 'at least we're rich in kids.'" Left to right in the front row are Maxine, Alice with Patty Victoria, Coach Saudargas with David, and Tommy. Standing in back are Shirley, Christine with Kelda, Alex Jr., Richard, and Jimmy.

After the Gym Goes Dark

While community organizations were besieging the Warriors, colleges across the country were besieging Coach Saudargas to head their basketball programs. Most were smaller colleges, but the University of Colorado also beckoned after his Warrior accomplishments were touted by a Denver radio station.

At the same time, Warrior prospects for a third straight state championship in 1957 looked good. Returning seniors included   6'6" Roger Peacock, 6'5" Jay Heath, 6'2" Chad Coffman, brother of the 1955 champions' guard Rod Coffman, and 5'10" Jack Flynn, who played a crucial role in the Warriors' Super-Sectional win over Galesburg. They were joined by 5'9 junior Bill Cacciatore, a future Northwestern University standout.

When sportswriters asked Coach Saudargas if he was going to stay at West High or become a college coach, he told them he was undecided. College coaching was appealing, he said, "if conditions were right." His foremost condition was enough income to meet his family's needs. None of the college offers measured up.

"I'm sure I could have done well," he told Rockford sportswriter Dave Albee later, "but the salaries were so lousy. They said, 'What about the prestige?' I asked, 'How much milk would prestige buy?'"

Grocery bills, utility bills, and medical bills were besieging Coach Saudargas even more relentlessly than colleges. Alice had undergone surgery for a precancerous condition the summer following the 1955 championship, adding to the medical bills from Patty Victoria's hospital care just four months earlier.

"Teachers didn't make much money, and we had no health insurance or benefits," Alice said. "What insurance we had he paid for with his side jobs selling cars at the Ford dealership or selling pots and pans door to door. We really struggled."

Dave McLaughlin, Warrior junior varsity basketball manager in 1955 and part-time produce manager at a National Tea grocery store in Rockford, said he would find Coach Saudargas waiting behind the store on Saturdays as the store closed for the weekend. That was when perishable vegetables and fruit not salable the following Monday were pitched.

"They were throwing them out," Alice said, "but they were perfectly good, so Alex would go there every Saturday afternoon late in the day and bring them home. We would eat them for a week. That was one of the ways we managed to stretch the budget."

It was the family budget that finally induced Coach Saudargas to give up coaching entirely and pursue what promised to be a more lucrative career in finance. "Alex was always worried about money," Alice said. "That's why he resigned from West in the summer and took a job selling securities for an investment company. It was a mistake. He was very trusting and believed people who told him how much money he would make with all his contacts and what a wonderful opportunity it was for us. But he was really engrossed in coaching and he really loved kids. Selling securities and investment portfolios was not the same."

He stayed with the investment company about a year, she said, "but he had no training for it, and it didn't work out. We were destitute then, so I went to work at W.T. Grants. I managed the women's department and was paid thirty-eight dollars every two weeks. Then we received a letter from the mortgage company saying we had so many weeks to catch up on payments or we would be out on the street. Alex went to a different lender and managed to get another mortgage so we could stay in our home."

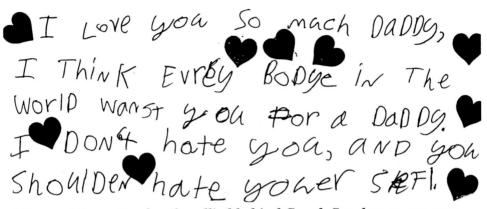

I Love you So mach DaDDy,
I Think Evrey Bodye iN The
worlD wanst you For a DaDDg.
I DoN4 hate you, aND you
ShoulDeN hate yoNer SEFl.

Alice and the entire family rallied behind Coach Saudargas any way
they could when he was snubbed and shunned by fair-weather friends.

During basketball season, Coach Saudargas earned a little extra income writing for Chicago newspapers and signing on as a commentator for state tournament telecasts. When he returned to Champaign to report on the 1957 championship games, his beloved Warriors were left behind. The Warriors had won the Rockford Regional Tournament but were eliminated in the Sterling Sectional, losing to Forreston 55-49 and finishing the season with 19 wins and five losses.

A few months later Coach Saudargas saw an opportunity to return to the world of education he loved when the Winnebago County Superintendent of Schools announced that he was retiring. "He decided to run for the office," Alice said. "At that time, the county was controlled by the Republican party and everyone needed party permission to run for office. Alex applied, but party bosses already had picked their own candidate. Alex decided to run anyway. He won the primary, but lost in the general election when party bosses he alienated in the primary threw their support behind another candidate.

"He ran for superintendent because he thought he could do a good job," Alice said, "but he was politically naive. He had no idea there was so much politics in the schools. What hurt him the most in the campaign was when he would walk along a street downtown and people who before had come up to him and glad-handed him and told him how wonderful he was and what a great job he had done in putting Rockford on the map as far as

Coach Saudargas' return to West was special edition headline news.

the state was concerned didn't know him anymore. He would greet them, but they would just walk by as if they didn't know he existed, or they would walk across the street to avoid running into him.

"It hurt him so deeply he never really got over it. He loved people, he loved everyone, and he felt they loved him back. He wouldn't treat anybody the way he was being treated, and he couldn't understand how anyone else could treat people that way. It was painful for him and painful for me. I would come home from work and find him sitting on the sofa in tears, just in tears, crying and crying and telling me how he had failed me as a husband and father to our children, how he felt so worthless and useless because he wasn't able to take care of us the way he wanted. He was close to a breakdown. All I could do was put my arms around him and tell him I loved him and his family loved him."

But that was not all Alice did. She took a job with the Winnebago County Sheriff's Department and began campaigning for her husband to return to teaching and coaching. "Sheriff Ivor Johnson offered me a job as a Deputy Sheriff working in the accounting department and going on calls whenever they needed a female to go out with them. It wasn't much money, but it was more than I was making at Grants."

Meanwhile former alderman Ben Schleicher, an ardent Warrior fan who attended all the West High basketball games and had traveled with the team to Champaign for the championships, was elected mayor. "That was when the Rockford school board was appointed by the mayor," Alice said, "so I called and asked him to help Alex get a job back in the school system. He told me, 'The powers-that-be say they'll never give him a job back here,' but I kept calling every few weeks and asking 'How are you? What are you doing for Alex?'

"After I talked to Ben about a dozen times, he finally said to me, 'Tell Alex to go over and see John Wise, the principal at Jefferson Junior High School.' Principals had the authority to hire whom they wanted at the time. Wise hired him immediately, but before Alex could start at Jefferson, Bob King, the Warrior coach who succeeded Alex, left West High for a college position. The principal at West, James Rose, wanted Alex, so that's how Alex got back into the school system."

After his three year exile in the world of money management and politics, Coach Saudargas finally was back home at West High doing the teaching and coaching he loved. He led his Warriors to Regional and Sectional Championships in 1965, 1966, 1967, 1969, 1973, and 1974, and to three finals in Champaign, but fell short of a third state championship. In 1966, the Warriors were eliminated in the first round. In 1967, his Warriors, led by all-conference picks Jim Sallis, Cal Glover, and Steve Amidon along with Cliff Partee and future Northwestern standout and Chicago Bulls draft pick Mark Sibley, went downstate with a 28-0 record, but lost their semifinal game 67-66 in overtime and finished fourth in the state. In 1973, the Warriors, led by Ernie Kent, all-conference, Parade magazine and Scholastic magazine All-American, and future NCAA coach, were defeated in the first round.

The clock ran out on his second term at the Warrior helm in 1976 when school politics took away Coach Saudargas' primary tools for teaching. Rockford's school board, disgruntled after voters rejected a tax increase referendum and facing a budget shortfall, decided to terminate high school athletics. With no sports program for teaching teamwork, goal-setting, self-discipline, resourcefulness, and other life skills central to his work with students, Coach Saudargas decided to retire.

After two terms totaling 26 years at West High, he left behind a basketball coaching legacy of two state championships, 28 Regional, Sectional, and Conference championships, and a tennis coaching legacy highlighted with a state championship by Dan Wikse, IHSA Boys Tennis Singles Champion in 1965, and three Big Eight Conference Tennis championships.

But his son Alex said his father's legacy far transcended winning championships. "Dad's greatest West High legacy was his love for his players — as though they were his own children. He wanted to see each of them succeed in life, and their education was very important to him. Dozens of kids who came from underprivileged homes never would have gone to college had it not been for my father finding scholarships for them. He did that day in and day out, relentlessly. It was a life mission for him.

State of Illinois
Presented to Alex Saudargas
as a token of our appreciation
for your patience, tolerance,
tutorage and guidance
when we thought we knew it
all. After twenty five years,
we realize we didn't!

With much gratitude
The West High Class of '55

West High's class of 1955 thanked Coach Saudargas for his work as coach and teacher with a handmade certificate at their 25th reunion.

"And his impact was felt throughout the community," he said. "Dad received a phone call from Johnny Wessels, who played for North Carolina State after graduating from West High and then transferred to the University of Illinois. He was working with Kinetico Water Systems in Rockford and told Dad about a black family, the Beasleys, who called him about a water softener.

"He said he stopped by their home, but it was late in the afternoon and Mrs. Beasley was preparing dinner. He offered to come back another time, but she told him to stay, then started calling the children to come in: 'Johnny, Bobby, Saudargas.' Wessels said, 'Saudargas?' She answered, 'Yeah, that's my youngest boy. When we watched Coach Saudargas with all those players, Bobby Washington, Nolden Gentry, Don Slaughter, we just thought he was the most wonderful man in the world, and I swore if I had another boy, I was going to name him Saudargas.'"

194

Alice said Coach Saudargas was loved as a teacher and was effective as a coach because "he took to heart a basic teaching tenet: 'Your students don't care what you know till they know that you care.' He truly cared about all his players, not only when they were playing for him, but all their lives. He would come home and talk about their exploits in college and in their careers and would send them notes telling them how proud he was of them."

Bob Washington said he felt that care during his years with the Warriors and later in life. After graduating from West High, Washington and two other 1956 Warrior stars, Nolden Gentry and Don Slaughter, enrolled at the University of Iowa. When Washington was caught up in an altercation triggered by racial taunts and slurs at an Iowa City bar, a man in the fight died. Washington was sentenced to prison, but continued his education there while he served out his term. Later he graduated from Iowa Wesleyan College with a degree in Sociology and was hired by the same prison as a counselor to help inmates stage comebacks in their lives.

"I went back to Rockford when the West High gym was dedicated in honor of Coach Saudargas," he said, "There was a Warriors' reunion gathering at Coach Saudargas' home. When he saw me coming down the steps and could see that everything was okay with me, he started crying. Yeah, he cared about us."

Coach Saudargas and Alice met in college and were married 58 years. "They were both big smilers yet gruff, but very good with people and tremendously persistent," said Rock River Times Editor and Publisher Frank Schier. "You never had to second guess either one of them. They believed in and fought for the common Joe and Jane."

The woman behind the man behind the championships

"Alice and Alex Saudargas stood side-by-side as champions of the children of West High, as warriors who made education the community's centerpiece. At the heart of Alice Saudargas' entire life has been community service and the nurturing of children: PTO when her own children were in school; her roles as teacher and principal; her leadership in Rockford's first Head Start program; her work on behalf of the citizens of Rockford. She calls to mind the image of a brave and stalwart soldier whose sense of purpose never wavers."

— Rockford City Council Proclamation
Celebrating her 95th birthday

Warriors Forever

Cultures Clash, Love Prevails

Coach Saudargas and Alice shared three lifelong passions: children, education, and each other. All three converged during the nearly three decades their family life was centered on West High School. All their children graduated from West High, and both Alex and Alice taught there.

Their passion for education first brought them together at Northern Illinois State Teachers College, now Northern Illinois University, during the Great Depression. Coach Saudargas was enrolled on a football scholarship to study physical education and zoology, Alice on an academic scholarship to study social science and botany.

"We met during freshman week when incoming students took IQ tests and signed up for classes," Alice said. "On the Friday night before classes started, there was a big mixer and, as usual, all the girls ended up on one side of the hall and all the boys on the other side. Alex finally walked over and asked me to dance. I didn't know much about dancing because I grew up on a farm, so I stepped all over his feet, but it didn't discourage him. Afterwards he told his football buddies, 'That's the girl I'm going to marry.'

"He kept asking me for a date, and I finally went out with him. We were sitting in a class together and he asked me what I was doing Saturday night. When I said, 'Nothing,' he asked me to a dance. What he didn't tell me was that he was supposed to go with another girl who was part of the group sponsoring the dance. When he tried to buy a ticket for us at the door, they were so angry with him they didn't want to sell him one. We finally got in, but it was embarrassing.

"Alex would hitchhike about 20 miles up the highway to see me at our family farm during summer breaks from classes. When we graduated in 1938, no teaching jobs were available, so he went on to the University of Illinois in Champaign for a Master's Degree in administration. I enrolled at a business college and got a job as a secretary in Rockford. That's when we decided to elope. He borrowed a car for our getaway to Iowa, but he wasn't familiar with the stick shift, so it was a very rough ride. We made it to Dubuque and were married there on Sunday, February 25, 1940."

More rough rides followed. Alex was the son of immigrant parents from a culture with rigidly defined roles for husband and wife. Alice was the daughter of a rebellious and independent mother who escaped from cultural constraints in Norway to pursue her interests and education in America. She was trained as a nurse and spoke fluent Norwegian, German, English, and French.

"Back then, women were supposed to be wives and mothers and housekeepers and caretakers of the children," Alice said. "In the home Alex came from, wives weren't supposed to have interests outside the home. It wasn't that way with me."

She challenged his expectations from the start. "I wanted to take a literature class the University of Illinois offered near our home, but Alex was against it. I found a way when we had a windstorm that wrecked the umbrella on our patio. I reported the damage to our insurance company, and the check we received turned out to be exactly the amount needed to pay for the course, so I went.

"When our first child, Christine was little, Alex would take her with him to his baseball games and horseshoe pitching with friends. The next thing I knew she was swearing. He and I had a little rendezvous about it and he realized it didn't sound good coming out of a little girl's mouth, so he cleaned up his language. We never had the problem again."

Alice also blew the whistle on Coach Saudargas when basketball invaded their bedroom "Alex never showed any emotion at the games," she said. "He would sit quietly and not scream and yell or shake his fist at the officials as some coaches do. After the games, the coaching staff and our friends would get together. Most of the time it was in our family room downstairs. My husband never drank and never smoked, but we had a well stocked bar and people loved to visit. They would talk about the game and replay it over and over again. After everybody left and we got all the stuff cleaned up, we'd go to bed.

"But sometimes Alex would still be thinking about the game and would dream about it through the night. He would toss and turn and flail his arms, and I would get punched and pushed and land on the floor. After a few seasons of that, I decided we needed a new mattress, a larger mattress, and made up my mind we were going to buy a new bedroom set.

"When we went to the furniture store, I never got a word in edgewise. He picked out what he thought we should have. The next day I called the salesman and canceled the order. Then I went to the store and picked out a king size bed and mattress because I was tired of landing on the floor.

"Alex resented that as an encroachment on his authority and wouldn't talk to me for months afterwards, but he eventually mellowed. What held us together through those kinds of tough times was our love, our commitment, but we had some knock-down-drag-out fights. I was so angry with him one night I locked the door so he couldn't get in. When I finally got up and let him in, we had this very long, heavy, heated discussion. I finally said to him, 'We can either grow old together, or you can go your way and I can go my way.' That was when the worm turned.

"We cared about each other and tried to help each other, and that's what made the difference. I was always very proud of what he was doing, and he was always very proud of what I was trying to do."

And she was proud of her family. "After a game at East High, I was talking with a friend whose husband taught there. A couple who didn't know me came over from the other end of the gym and broke into our conversation. The woman said to my friend, 'Did you hear the news? Mrs. Saudargas is expecting another baby. Isn't that awful?' She kept on talking till I finally became so angry I said to her, 'I wish you people would please get out of our bedroom. You're not supporting them. We are. That's our business, not your business. Get out of our bedroom and stay out.'"

Alice said her homemaker role as mother of 10 was dominant while their children were young, and it was her best preparation for meeting challenges she faced in her pursuits outside the home when they were older. "One of the things about Mom," their son Richard said, "was that she was always supportive of Dad, but she was also smart and capable in her own right."

She demonstrated that when Coach Saudargas was having financial troubles after the championship seasons and she worked as a department store manager and deputy sheriff. When she was asked to serve as Winnebago County campaign manager for the Nixon presidential campaign, she carried the county for him.

Later Alice applied as a teacher in the Rockford School District, "but they wouldn't hire me," she said, "because they were concerned that my family responsibilities might interfere with my attendance. Instead, they said I should apply as a substitute teacher.

"When I applied as a substitute teacher, the person in charge asked if I would consider substituting in special education. I said, 'Sure, it doesn't make any difference to me. Kids are kids.' Right away I received a three week assignment with a class of what were then called educable mentally handicapped children at Ellis School. I found them delightful.

"Then they sent me to another long term assignment with educable mentally handicapped children at Freeman School. I was there about five weeks when the person in charge praised my work and asked if I would like it to be a permanent job. I said I would. During the next couple summers, I went back to Northern Illinois University and became certified in special education.

"It was tough because at that time all teachers, not just special education teachers, didn't have lunch periods or time allotted to go to the bathroom. When the children ate, you ate. When the children went to the bathroom, you went to the bathroom. When the children went out to the playground, you went out to the playground. You were with them every single moment. The teachers' union finally negotiated with the district to get some private time for teachers during the school day."

She taught for the next 10 years while she continued summer studies at Northern Illinois University, earning a masters degree in administration. "I became what they called a troubleshooter," she said. "In

1969, Superintendent Arthur Johnson assigned me to West High to work with a group of unruly students even though Alex kept telling him, 'No, she's not coming over here.' He was afraid I would get hurt. The racial and ethnic friction that was sweeping the nation had infected the students, and there were fights in the school yard among West High students and with students who came over from other schools.

"I was escorted to a room with a locked door and a teacher inside with a group of students. When the teacher unlocked the door to let me in, I found students on the floor shooting craps and playing cards, but no learning going on. One huge student walked over to me and said, 'Get her out of here. Get Big Mama out of here. I don't want her in here.' I looked him in the eye and said, 'For your information, Big Mama is Mrs. Saudargas, and she is here to stay. You back off.' He eyeballed me for a while, then turned around and walked away, so I knew I had it made. There were other challenges, including a girl who put a razor blade to my throat until I calmed her down and we could talk. When I refused to show any fear, she and the others eventually came around.

"One thing they all had in common was that they couldn't read past a third grade level. And they had no coping mechanism. They didn't know how to cope with adversity if they ran into a problem, and they didn't know how to make good decisions. They couldn't figure out that if I do this, something bad can happen, or if I go another way, something good can happen. This is bad, this is good, they had never been taught how to make a good decision. Those were the things we had to work on with them.

"I laid down some rules and we did behavior modification, girls in one room, boys in another. They earned points if they did their lessons, sat in their seat, were quiet, and didn't bother their neighbor. Every Friday afternoon those who earned enough points were taken on an outing as a reward. The ones who didn't earn enough points had to stay behind and work. I can tell you, the next week they were ready to go.

"I was there for two years and wrote a teaching program for them which I refined during my next assignment as principal of the Boys Farm School in Durand, a facility for disruptive boys ages 13 to 17. I set the tone for the school, as I did for all the schools where I was made principal. I sat down with each class the first day of school and told them we were a family. I didn't stand up, I sat down so I was at their level. I told them school was their job, that just as parents go to a job, this is your job. Your teacher is taking the place of your mother or father. If there are any problems, go talk to your teacher, or you can come down and talk to me and we'll see what we can do because we're your family. That was the emphasis. I did that in every school with the teachers and students so they all felt that we were their family, their home, and somebody cared about them. We never had any graffiti problems, never had any thievery. It was great, but it was hard work."

Alice continued working in the schools for ten years after Alex retired, moving on from the Boys Farm School to serve as principal at Elmwood Center, Wight Elementary School, and Nashold Elementary School. "I would visit classes each day to see how things were going, then, after the kids would leave and the staff would leave, I'd stay and do all my paperwork, so it would be 6 or 7 o'clock before I'd leave the building to go home. Alex was understanding and supportive."

She kept up that pace until retiring in 1986, but not before helping launch a Head Start program in Rockford, despite opposition by local leaders, to give disadvantaged children and victims of discrimination more opportunities to succeed. At the same time, she served on the Winnebago County Child Protection Agency and the Council for Exceptional Children and wrote programs for drug and alcohol education, health education, and parenting.

It was as Alice was preparing to step down that West High's gym was named in honor of Coach Saudargas, the high point of his retirement years, but more challenges followed for both. "Alex absolutely would not go to a doctor, even though his health was declining," Alice said. "He was very athletic all of his life and thought that was going to carry him, but it didn't. I would make a doctor's appointment for him, but he wouldn't go. Finally he had a minor stroke on the golf course, but even that did not change him. When he was sent to a cardiologist afterwards, he walked in and said, 'I don't know what I'm doing here. I'm fine. Nothing's wrong.' He ended up having a quadruple bypass. Later he was diagnosed with diabetes.

"We were devastated in 1989 when the Rockford Board of Education used a district budget deficit to justify closing West High

School, but I really think the turning point as far as my husband's health was concerned came in June of 1990," Alice said. "I was making lunch when the phone rang. It was our daughter, Patty, but she didn't want to talk to me. She wanted to talk to her father. I could tell by the tone of her voice that something was very, very wrong and I wouldn't get off the phone. She finally told me and I just screamed and screamed and screamed. Alex got on the phone and she told him that our daughter Kelda and her husband were killed in a car crash in Arizona and their three children were in the Children's Hospital in Phoenix.

"I immediately got on the phone to make arrangements for us to fly out. When we arrived, our oldest granddaughter, Sheila, who was badly injured, looked at me and said, 'Grandma, I thought you and Grandpa would be dead before my Mommy and Daddy. Who's going to take care of us now? Who's going to want three orphans?' It just tore our hearts out. Alex never got over that.

"We tried to keep all the children together with an aunt and uncle, but one of our granddaughters was badly traumatized and needed special care. She came to live with us because I was trained to help trauma victims cope with loss. It was difficult, but she began doing well in high school and went on to excel in college.

In 1997, Alice was asked to fill a vacancy on the Rockford School Board when the District C board member died. She agreed to serve the remainder of the term and then to run for the full term in the next election. Before that election, Alex suffered a severe stroke and Alice decided to withdraw. She wrote a letter explaining her decision:

"Up until December 5, 1998, I had fully intended to run for office in District C. The events of December 5 changed all that. Alex suffered a disabling stroke which has long-term, uncertain outcomes. I have had to reassess my priorities and commitments. Without question, my husband, my partner in life for nearly 59 years, is most important to me, as is our family. This community and its children are a very close second. It is with deep regret that I cannot be a candidate for the school board election seat in District C. Life is a gift, and it is fragile. I need to be there for him and my family. As time permits, I shall continue to work to move this community and its schools forward. I thank each of you for all your prayers and support."

Alice was with Coach Saudargas constantly in the days ahead. "It is difficult to watch somebody that you love and has been your partner through all the ups and downs of a wonderful life, to watch him go inch by inch. He died about two months later, on March 1. As you get older, you not only get closer, but you also get a little bit more dependent on each other. I'll never forget his saying to me after the kids were all married and gone, 'Alice, we've just got each other now.' But now I don't have him. I'm alone, and it's tough. I sat on the couch for weeks on end after he passed away. I just couldn't move."

"Alex 'is' West High"

"My best memory of West High School is my last, at the farewell reception when the school was closed. There amid a sea of mostly unfamiliar faces, near the center of that grand old gymnasium named in his honor, stood 'the man,' Alex Saudargas. The warm glow of his magnetic smile, the ever-present bow tie; to me, Alex 'is' West High. He symbolizes all that is good and great about the school. Warrior pride lives on forever!"

— Gary Williams, Rockford, Class of '59.

West High School was a training ground for champions, including state championships in Girls Field Hockey, IHSA Boys Tennis, and multiple state championships in swimming and golf. Conference, district, regional, and state championship plaques and trophies filling walls and display cases testify to Warrior excellence in academics and the arts as well as in sports — including state championships in debate and state honors in speech and drama.

Warriors Forever

Rockford school board's decision to close West High School cast a shadow over graduation day, 1989. West's final graduating class chose to dispel the gloom by inviting Nolden Gentry to deliver the school's last commencement address.

Because Gentry played a central role in West High's championship seasons, his presence hearkened back to the school's brightest days and Rockford's proudest moments. Gentry also personified both the spirit of West High and the legacy of Coach Saudargas.

He was "the real driving force behind my team," Coach Saudargas wrote in a sports column for the Chicago Daily News after the championship seasons. "Without peer as a rebounder and feeder, he held the boys together and scored key points when the chips were down." Gentry received all-state, all-tournament, and all-conference honors during his West High years, and won national recognition when he, along with future NBA pro hall-of-famer Oscar Robinson, was chosen for the nation's All-American High School Team in a poll of college and professional coaches, scouts, and sportswriters by the Newspaper Enterprise Association. He was inducted into the Illinois Basketball Coaches Hall of Fame in 1973.

Athlete/scholar Gentry also embodied the passion for education shared by both Coach Saudargas and Alice. He served as president of the National Honor Society at West High and passed up a professional basketball career after graduating from the University of Iowa where he was a Hawkeye varsity star for three years. He chose instead to earn a Doctor of Law degree from the university's law school. Finding few opportunities for black lawyers in the 1960s, he worked with the FBI on the East Coast briefly before becoming an Assistant Attorney General for the State of Iowa and settling in DesMoines. Later he joined with other attorneys as a founding partner in a private law firm there.

Echoing a goal-setting mantra of Coach Saudargas, Gentry told graduates, "As you prepare for your next step, start with the development of a plan outlining your dreams and aspirations for the future and the efforts you are willing to invest in your success.

"Once you have locked in on your dream, focus on the effort needed to make your dream a reality — effort that is more than what is expected, effort that is more than what you are paid or rewarded for, effort that is more than others are putting forth. That kind of effort gives you focus, intensity, and magnetism — intensity to stay on track and magnetism to attract others to your dream."

He thanked Coach Saudargas, "who kept reminding us that basketball, in the final analysis, is only a game," and he told the graduates, "Success in life is surely not an external thing. It comes not from money, fame, people, power, nor even knowledge. It must come from within, from making hard choices, daring to differ from your peers, all of which require strength of will, strength of character, strength of conviction and all of which are qualities that come from within."

Those qualities of quiet courage were imbued in Gentry and his Warrior championship teammates by Coach Saudargas. They fueled Gentry's personal success and sustained him when he took a stand against discrimination in DesMoines schools and housing — akin to the lifelong fight waged in Rockford by Coach Saudargas and Alice. In 2005, Gentry was awarded the University of Iowa Distinguished Alumni Award for his service on the boards of more than two dozen community organizations and businesses. In 2007, he was inducted into the Iowa African American Hall of Fame for his role as the first African American to serve on the

DesMoines Board of Education and for his ability to advance desegregation by bringing together factions with divergent views.

In Rockford, with the closing of West High School, the struggle to end desegregation was just beginning.

Rockford newspaper columnist Pat Cunningham warned that the closing of West High School would be "seen as callous and promulgated by an East Side power structure that is insensitive to, if not disdainful of the West Side... It does no good to deny that it sometimes carries a racial component... It may also involve a political and social estrangement that is much more bitter, widespread, and enduring."

As Cunningham had predicted, closing West High School triggered community outrage and division lasting well into the twenty-first century. It ultimately led to a citizens' coalition known as People Who Care and court action that exposed systemic segregation in Rockford's public schools and a broader culture of discrimination, both blatant and subtle, that created and tolerated it. Alice soon found herself in the middle of efforts to overcome and rectify the discrimination she and Coach Saudargas had been grappling with for decades.

Her efforts were interrupted a few months after the death of Coach Saudargas when she was mugged in a grocery store parking lot. "The bones in her shoulder shattered when she hit the ground," Rockford newspaper columnist Judy Emerson said. "She underwent five and a half hours of surgery to rebuild her shoulder with bone grafts and plastic parts. Saudargas has not had a pain-free day since the teens knocked her down and stole her purse,"

It would be natural for a victim to denounce her attackers, Emerson said, but Alice, "who spent much of her life trying to rescue 'throwaway kids,'" was thinking more about the muggers than about herself. "'I feel sorry for those kids,' Alice said. 'If there is not the impetus at home to provide discipline and supervision, then the school district has to do something. I still want to be really involved with school issues rather than flat on my back,' For one thing, she'd like to see more educational opportunities for troubled kids like the ones who attacked her."

It wasn't long before Alice was involved again. In the spring of 2000, she published a letter rebuking the school board for its handling of the People Who Care lawsuit and for spending more than a million dollars in four months on lawyers' fees which contributed nothing to improving children's education. "As a taxpayer and former school board member, I am outraged at the amount of dollars the latest round of litigation cost taxpayers," she said as she called for a negotiated settlement of the lawsuit. "The fund that pays legal fees will soon be out of money. I fear the fund responsible for ongoing district operations will be raided to pay for legal costs," and she called the board's actions "counterproductive — not only for the taxpayers, but for the students."

In the next election, she won a seat on the school board, bringing to the office decades of experience as a teacher and principal and, at age 84, holding the distinction of being the most senior school board member in Illinois. She served two terms, from 2003 to 2011. As both she and Alex had done all their lives, she used her years on the school board to expand educational opportunities for all children in every part of the community — and she acquired a reputation for being blunt, outspoken, abrasive, and confrontational in the process. Adversaries soon learned that coming between Alice and the interests of the children was like coming between a mother bear and her cubs.

She remained committed to the end, accepting a citizen coalition's draft to come out of retirement and run for the school board again in 2013. Opponents kept her off the ballot by challenging her petitioners' signatures and scheduling a hearing on the petitions while she was hospitalized and unable to attend. She requested a hearing to confirm signature validity with affidavits when she was released from the hospital, but her request was denied. When supporters then launched a write-in campaign on her behalf, sponsors of candidate forums refused to let her participate in school issue debates at the forums. Despite those obstacles, she won 15 percent of the vote.

Alice continued working to influence school board decisions with letters and commentaries up to her death two years later, on June 8, 2015, at age 99. "Alice Saudargas embodied what's best in Rockford" was the headline on the Rockford Register Star editorial page the following morning. "You could always count on Alice Saudargas to cut through whatever baloney a school administration was trying to feed the public and make sure students were the primary concern. She and her husband Alex were influential in the region for more than seven decades."

In his commencement address to the members of West High School's final graduating class, Nolden Gentry encouraged them to set worthy goals and aspire to personal and professional achievement. It marked the end of West High School, but not of the indomitable Warrior spirit encapsulated in Gentry's speech and enshrined in the lives of Coach Saudargas and Alice: "strength of will, strength of character, strength of conviction" coupled with "effort that is more than what is expected, effort that is more than what you are paid or rewarded for, effort that is more than others are putting forth" — the spirit of Warriors Forever.

A man of the century

Rockford's daily newspaper, the Register Star, cited Coach Saudargas as one of the city's foremost achievers in its review of twentieth-century highlights: "The trademark bow ties, the military-issue haircut, the out-of-date glasses, and the back-to-back victories among five trips to the state basketball championships all conspired to make Saudargas a coaching legend. When he died in March of 1999 at 82, former players and community leaders galore filed past his casket on the baseline beneath one of the hoops in the West gym, which long before had been named in his honor."

Warriors Forever

Afterthoughts

Few knew of the personal and political adversity Coach Saudargas and Alice weathered before, during, and after the championship seasons or of their health troubles and their near financial ruin. Most knew only of their unwavering commitment to West High School in particular, to education in general, and to the well-being of the students and athletes they encouraged and empowered to set and achieve personal goals.

"It was unbelievable," said younger son Richard Saudargas, "to see the number of Warriors from all over the country who came back for the visitation and for the funeral memorial service when Dad passed away. We're talking 50 years later, a long span of time. They recognized that he had a lifetime impact on them, and they were grateful."

Coach Saudargas, Gentry, and Wessels were inducted into the Illinois Basketball Coaches Hall of Fame individually for their personal achievements. They were joined by all their teammates when the 1956 state championship squad was inducted with team honors in 1974 and the 1955 state champions were inducted eight years later.

On the following pages in alphabetical order are Coach Saudargas' 1955 and 1956 Warriors with descriptions of the roles they played on the teams and an overview of what they went on to do later in their lives.

Luther Bedford
Reserve guard 1955
B. S. Illinois Wesleyan University
M. S. Governor State University
Teacher, Coach, Athletic Director
Marshall High School
Chicago, Illinois

Sam Black
Reserve forward 1955
B. S. Mechanical Engineering
University of Wisconsin
B. S. Naval Science
University of Wisconsin
Lt. Colonel, U. S. Marines, 21 year career
Sweden, Maine

Tom Blake
Starting guard 1956
Attended Bradley University
Thirty years with J. I. Case Company
Retired as Plant Manager, Quad Cities
Rockford, Illinois

Fred Boshela
Starting forward 1955
Attended Iowa State University
General Contractor – Owner
Garland, Texas

Roscoe Burke,
Reserve guard 1956
B. A. Jackson State College
Twenty-five years with Chrysler Corporation
Rockford, Illinois

Chad Coffman
Reserve forward 1956
Attended Bethany Junior College
B. S. Parson College
Probation Officer and Police Officer
Rockford, Illinois

Rod Coffman
Starting guard 1955
Attended Bethany College
Owner of the Gilroy Garlic Company
Later sold to the McCormick Spice Company
Monte Sereno, California

Joe DiGiovanni
Reserve center 1955
Businessman and Entrepreneur
Branch manager Wonder Bread/Hostess Cake
Kishwaukee Tavern & Rocky's Tap
Rockford, Illinois

Jack Flynn
Reserve guard 1956
Attended Drake University
B. S. Northern Michigan University
M. S. University of New Mexico
Teacher and Coach, Guilford High School
Rockford, Illinois

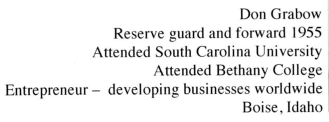

Nolden Gentry
Starting forward 1955 and 1956
B. S. University of Iowa
J. D. University of Iowa
Special Agent for the F. B. I.
Assistant Attorney General,
Iowa Department of Justice
Private Law Practice
Des Moines, Iowa

Don Grabow
Reserve guard and forward 1955
Attended South Carolina University
Attended Bethany College
Entrepreneur – developing businesses worldwide
Boise, Idaho

Jay Heath
Reserve forward 1956
Attended Drake University
B. A. Northern Michigan University
J. D. University of Illinois
Attorney and GM Industrial Relations,
LTV Railroads in Pittsburgh & Cleveland
Rockford, Illinois

221

Dave McClelland

David McClelland
Reserve center 1955
B. S. University of Illinois
D. D. S. University of Illinois
Practiced in Rockford more than 40 years
Rockford, Illinois

Ray Morgan
Reserve guard 1955
B. S. Illinois Wesleyan University
M. S. Southern Illinois University
Employed by IBM more than 30 years
Worked throughout the country
Retired in Atlanta, Georgia

Tom Olson
Reserve forward 1955
Attended the University of Illinois
B. S. Rockford College
Served in the U. S. Marines
Vice President of Amcore Bank
Rockford, Illinois

Warriors Forever

Rex Parker
Starting guard 1955
B. S. Illinois State University
M.B.A. Northern Illinois University
VP & GM Clock Tower Resort
Assistant Professor Rock Valley College
Rockford, Illinois

Sam Patton
Reserve guard , 1955 and 1956
Attended the University of Illinois
Manufacturing plant manager
Kimberline, Missouri

Roger Peacock
Reserve center 1956
B. S. University of Colorado
M. S. University of Denver
Systems Analyst
Oak Ridge, Tennessee

Craig Peeples
Reserve forward 1956
B. S. DePauw University
Real Estate Appraiser
Retired Lt. Colonel Air Force Reserve
Polson, Montana

Don Slaughter
Starting forward 1956, reserve forward 1955
Attended University of Iowa
B. S. University of California, Berkley
M. S. University of California, Berkley
Assistant professor at San Jose State University
Human Resource Manager at Stanford University
Palo Alto, California

Tom Urnezis
Reserve guard 1956
Professional Degree in Banking
Twenty-five years with Alpine Bank
President of Alpine Bank
Chairman of the Board of Alpine Bank
Rockford, Illinois

Robert "Bobby" Washington
Starting guard 1956, reserve guard 1955
Attended University of Iowa
B. A. Iowa Wesleyan
Attended Mankato State University as a graduate
student
Worked for Iowa Department of Corrections
Burlington, Iowa

John "Johnny" Wessels
Starting center 1955 and 1956
Attended University of North Carolina State
University of Illinois
Sales & Sales Management
Kinetico Water Systems
Rockford, Illinois

"You may not always be able to control results, but you can always control your effort," was Coach Saudargas' counsel for his Warriors facing challenges on the hardwood. "The clock may run out on you, but you never lose if you never quit."

Johnny Wessels, last on the alphabetical roster but usually first in Warrior scoring and a perpetual fan favorite, reflected that spirit in everything he did. After graduating from West High and playing briefly for North Carolina State University, Wessels transferred to the University of Illinois, joining with Manny Jackson and Govonor Vaughn, two Edwardsville greats he played against in the 1956 championship game. He starred from 1958 through 1961 with the Fighting Illini and was nominated for All-Big 10 honors. Afterwards he was chosen in the NBA draft by the Chicago Majors. When his basketball-playing years ended, he went on to win national awards in his sales career.

Wessels' greatest challenge came when he was diagnosed with cancer in his early 50s. As Coach Saudargas was leaving the hospital at the end of their final visit, Wessels' last words to him were, "I'm going to beat this, Coach." He was still fighting when the clock ran out on him in December, 1994, at the age of 56. Always a Warrior, Wessels never quit.